ENCOUNTERING THE UNEXPLAINED

Human beings have been having encounters with the unexplained ever since they first began thinking about the mysteries of life, death, the Universe and everything. Every culture around the world has its own stories of powerful deities or terrifying demons, its beliefs in a spirit realm complete with ghostly inhabitants, and its folklore concerning mischievous fairies, monstrous creatures or bizarre entities apparently not of this world.

While some would argue that the kinds of encounters found in such traditions should be relegated to the status of legends and old wives' tales, people continue to have inexplicable and sometimes frightening experiences, even today. Drawing the line between objective and subjective reality has always been problematic, and to dismiss such experiences as hallucinations or delusions is to fail to engage with the seemingly inexhaustible strangeness of the human condition.

For the last 35 years, *Fortean Times* magazine has been reporting on the world of strange phenomena – and for 35 years our readers have been telling us of their own odd experiences in letters and emails from all over the world. Some of these stories are scary, some are funny, some are mystifying and some are just downright weird, but they are all accounts of events that have actually happened to people – from living in a haunted house to witnessing a rain of frogs, from experiencing a timeslip to seeing your own double.

We haven't tried to explain the many odd and unnerving tales contained in this collection – we leave you to arrive at your own conclusions – but we've certainly enjoyed sharing them. We hope you do too.

David Sutton, Editor, Fortean Times

It Happened To Me!

REAL-LIFE TALES OF THE PARANORMAL
VOLUME 1

Ordinary people's extraordinary stories from the pages of FORTEAN TIMES

EDITED AND COMPILED BY
Paul Sieveking and Jen Ogilvie

DESIGN AND PHOTOGRAPHY
Etienne Gilfillan

COVER IMAGE
David Newton

EDITOR IN CHIEF
David Sutton

PUBLISHING & MARKETING
Simon Davies
020 7907 6369/6193
simon_davies@dennis.co.uk

BOOKAZINE MANAGER
Dharmesh Mistry
020 7907 6100
dharmesh_mistry@dennis.co.uk

DENNIS PUBLISHING LTD

DIRECTOR OF ADVERTISING: Julian Lloyd-Evans
NEWSTRADE DIRECTOR: Martin Belson
FINANCE DIRECTOR: Brett Reynolds
GROUP FINANCE DIRECTOR: Ian Leggett
CHIEF EXECUTIVE: James Tye
CHAIRMAN: Felix Dennis

Printed in England by BGP Print Ltd, Chaucer International Estate, Launton Road, Bicester, Oxon OX6 7QZ
Distribution Seymour Distribution 020 7396 8000

IT HAPPENED TO ME! VOLUME 1 is published by Dennis Publishing Ltd, 30 Cleveland Street, London W1T 4JD, a company registered in England number 1138891. Entire contents copyright 2008 Dennis Publishing Ltd.

PERMISSIONS AND REPRINTS
Material in It Happened To Me! Volume 1 may not be reproduced in any form without the publisher's written permission. It is available for licensing overseas.

For details contact Winnie Liesenfeld, Publishing Services Manager: 020 7907 6134
winnie_liesenfeld@dennis.co.uk

HOW TO CONTACT US
MAIL: 30 Cleveland Street, London W1T 4JD
PHONE: 020 7907 6000
EMAIL AND WEB
Website: www.forteantimes.com
Letters for publication: BOX 2409 London NW5 4NP, sieveking@forteantimes.com

To contact advertising:
James Clements 020 7907 6724
james_clements@dennis.co.uk

Change your address, open or renew a subscription or report any problems at www.subsinfo.co.uk 0844 844 0049

It Happened To Me!
REAL-LIFE TALES OF THE PARANORMAL

ORDINARY PEOPLE'S EXTRAORDINARY STORIES FROM THE PAGES OF **FORTEAN TIMES**

CONTENTS

CHAPTER 1   P8

HIGH SPIRITS
Haunted houses and ghostly encounters

CHAPTER 2   P26

DON'T PANIC!
Nameless dreads and sudden terrors

CHAPTER 3   P40

DOUBLE TROUBLE
Doppelgängers and impostors

CHAPTER 4   P52

THE SIXTH SENSE
Premonitions and portents of death

CHAPTER 5   P64

TIMESLIPS
Historical visions and temporal anomalies

CHAPTER 6   P76

OUT OF THE BLUE
Showers of fish and rains of snails

CHAPTER 7   P86
STRANGE CREATURES
Monsters and mysterious animals

CHAPTER 8   P100
THE LITTLE PEOPLE
Meetings with fairies and pixies

CHAPTER 9   P110
DOWN THE LINE
Telephone calls from the other side

CHAPTER 10   P120
ON THE ROAD
Terrifying trips on haunted highways

CHAPTER 11   P132
HEARING THINGS
Spooky sounds and spectral music

CHAPTER 12   P144
THE TWILIGHT ZONE
Tales of high strangeness

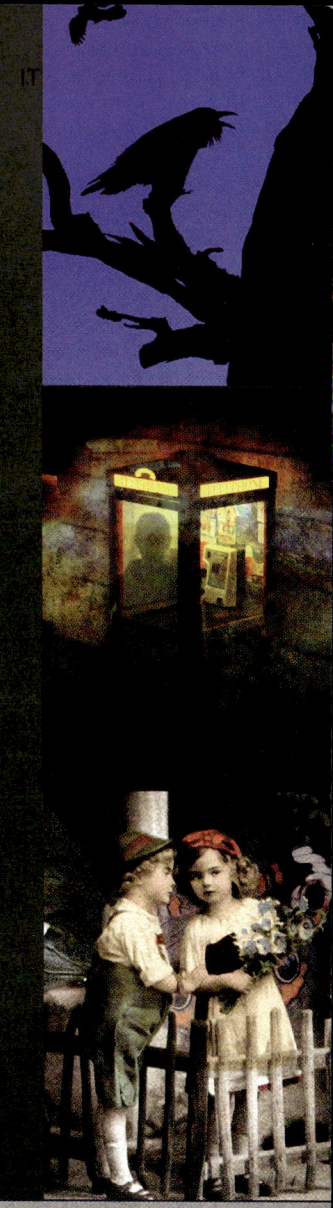

1 High Spirits

The world's shadows seethe with spectres of all kinds, from evil baby-killing ghouls to departed family members popping back to say hello. Whether it's a phantom monk preaching from the other side, a Nazi wraith stalking a bombed-out building, a ghostly young nun wailing in a chapel, or troubled spirits haunting spooky old houses, everyone, it seems, has a ghost story to tell...

HAUNTED HOUSES

THE SPOOK OF SMITH SQUARE

In 1949, when I was 17, I worked at the headquarters of the United Europe Movement, an organisation founded by Winston Churchill – the start of the modern EEC. My role was junior "dogsbody": running messages, sending off post, making tea and other such tasks.

The offices were housed in an elegant Queen Anne house, Number One, Smith Square, not far from the Houses of Parliament.

One morning I was just about to make coffee when I noticed a stranger sitting in the inner room, which had been partitioned from the large one where I worked. He was wearing a long black robe and cloak, and a hat which resembled an upturned soup plate.

"Shall I make that gentleman a cup of coffee?" I quietly asked one of the other girls, Jeanne Dawkins.

"What gentleman?"

I pointed and whispered: "The one in there. He looks like a priest."

"I haven't seen anyone."

Deciding to enquire of the stranger himself, I peeped into the room. There was no one there. All the time I had been able to see whether anyone came in or out.

9

It was puzzling.

"That's funny," I said, "I could have sworn I saw a priest. He looked just like the label on a bottle of Sandeman's port..."

The next day, Rosemary Streeter, who worked in the room upstairs, came into our office shaking uncontrollably, her face as white as paper. Eventually, she managed to tell us that she had been coming down the magnificent marble staircase to give us some documents when a foreign-looking priest passed her.

She'd looked over her shoulder to say "Good morning" and the man had simply vanished! "He looked like the picture on a bottle of Sandeman's," she said.

After that, there was no stopping "Charlie Harry" as he became known. We never saw an actual form again, but the lights would suddenly go out and come back on, doors wouldn't open because of heavy pressure being exerted from within, objects flew about the room, there were whooshes of cold air, and we heard weird, far-away voices. It became frightening, to the extent that none of us would venture alone into the passage or beyond.

We went to see our boss, Brian Goddard, about it. He was not at all surprised because he already knew about the ghost. So did Churchill's son-in-law, Duncan Sandys (Mr Goddard's direct superior) and others.

"There's nothing to worry about. He's been doing it for years. He won't hurt you..."

Won't hurt you, indeed! The last straw came one day when a sudden, violent force barged into me and shunted me at speed across the room into a corner. I hit the wall and sank to the floor. My nose was bleeding, although I hadn't knocked it. The rest of the girls ran, screaming, from the room and I fainted. The next thing I knew, everyone was standing round me looking scared out of their wits.

I left my job within a week. In time, I lost contact with my fellow-workers, and memories of the priest began to fade. But I still sometimes wonder why Charlie Harry took a dislike to me.

Josephine Taylor, Hastings, East Sussex, 1996

LADY IN BLACK

Lectures that morning had swept from the dark satanic mills up to just before the Great War. I had followed this with some two hours quiet study in the University Library. It was November, and by about three in the afternoon I returned to my lodgings in Sutton Coldfield in the West Midlands.

“ I turned round and there stood a little old lady dressed from head to toe in black… ”

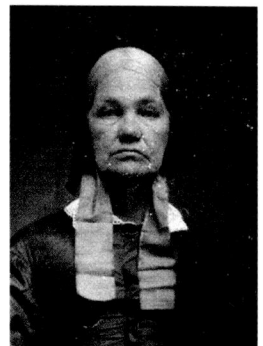

Mrs Branksome, my landlady, was a 76-year-old widow who put up with me more for company and to have a man about the house than for the rent I was able to pay her. I had just completed five years' war service and was catching up on those lost years with a degree course at Birmingham. It would be fair to say that I had both feet firmly on the ground and was not given to daydreaming or idle speculation.

As I put my latch-key into the front door I knew Mrs Branksome was out and that I would have the house to myself for some hours. It was still daylight, but rapidly darkening, when I slid the door catch and entered the house, swinging round through the door with my back to the stairs while I removed the key from the lock. The stairs swept up out of the hall, with two small landings at each turn up to the first floor. As I closed the door, I knew instantly that I was not alone. I turned round to face the stairs and there, some 20ft (6m) away on the first landing, stood a little old lady, dressed from head to toe in black bombazine. She smiled at me, I drew a deep breath and then she was gone. I blinked, shook my head and wondered just what or whom I had seen. Strangely, I felt no fear, just an overwhelming feeling of being welcome. When Mrs Branksome returned that evening, we had our usual evening chat and that was that.

Some three weeks later my landlady invited me into her kitchen and we shared a late cup of chocolate and sat before her open coal fire. She suddenly tapped me on the knee and, casting her cat-green eyes into mine, said: "Come on John, tell me all about it."

"Tell you about what?" "You've seen mother, haven't you?"

I said that I did not know what on earth she was talking about; whereupon she rose, went over to her kitchen table and, opening a small drawer, withdrew a photograph of the old lady I had seen up the stairs.

"When did you see her?" she asked.

"About three weeks ago, one afternoon when I returned from college. I haven't mentioned it because I did not want to alarm you."

"Mother told me she had seen you," she said, "so you would not have alarmed me. She left us 40 years ago, but she still likes to know who's in the house."

John Birch, Saundersfoot, Dyfed, 1997

BROTHER DOLLY

We appear to be haunted by a friendly monk who is almost like one of the family. We have called him Brother Adolphus (Brother Dolly for short). I have seen him on three occasions; my adult daughter, Adrienne, once; and my 13-year-old Down's Syndrome son Jean-Paul claims to see him quite often. Even when he is not visible we are aware of his presence. Brother Dolly walks the landing and the staircase and most nights we hear his footsteps. Sometimes he lifts the latch on the bedroom door as if about to enter, then thinks better of it.

In October 1998, a stain in the shape of a cross materialised over the mantelpiece in our sitting room. On 2 January this year, after a few days' holiday, we came home to discover writing on the wall of the sitting room. The word is *tangnefedd*, which we have discovered is an Old Welsh word for peace. It is usually used in a religious context and is seldom heard today.

As you can imagine, we find all this activity intriguing. Our pet monk's presence is totally benign and the farmhouse exudes a warm friendly atmosphere.

Rose-Mary Gower, Mold, Flintshire, 1999

There has been some extraordinary activity in our house since my last letter. The first word to appear on the wall was *tangnefedd* (peace). This was followed at regular intervals by about 20 other words, all in Welsh and mostly of a religious nature. None are threatening. The words appear as a brown stain, slightly darker than the paintwork. Some have almost appeared before our eyes; one minute they were definitely not there, the next they were. Others have materialised slowly over days or weeks.

Brother Doli (he prefers the Welsh spelling to 'Dolly') is very much in evidence. We have his self-portrait on a stone at the top of our staircase with the word *mynach* (monk) carved on it (see photo). The figure appeared one day and the carving several days later. However, the lettering does not look new, but seems worn, as if it had been there for years. A cross over our mantelpiece appeared last October, but comes and goes at intervals. Recently, it has been joined by four other crosses and a stain resembling a ninth-century Celtic chalice. These also appear as brown marks on the stonework. A Christian symbol – a P running through an X – appeared in a couple of places on the wall and fireplace in June.

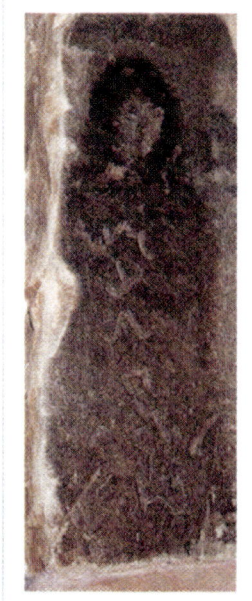

John-Paul says he sees Doli all the time in his bedroom and is trying to teach him to play Nintendo. After a recent short holiday, John-Paul went straight upstairs to play Nintendo and was decidedly put out when Doli stood in front of the TV screen so he couldn't see what he was doing. We came to the conclusion that this was our monk's way of saying welcome home. When he was acknowledged, Doli went back into his usual place by John-Paul's bed and normal play resumed. On two occasions I have felt someone sit on the end of the bed and shuffle around until comfortable. It was light enough to see that there was no one there. I assumed it was Doli.

He is a sensitive soul. If a joke is made about his presence, he responds very quickly with another word or cross! This seems to be done in a slightly reproachful tone. After making a disparaging comment about our spook, my husband David woke up one morning to find himself in a pair of underpants different from the ones he was wearing when he got into bed. We eventually found his boxer shorts neatly laundered and back in his underwear drawer. We also found the word *mynach* embossed on some papers he was working on.

In March 1999 we were visited by a Welsh sensitive who claimed to be able to communicate with Doli. He said a mounted soldier killed our monk with a sword on the nearby riverbank in 1613. Doli thought he was too young to die and wanted to do some good in the world. He felt our family would be receptive towards him. The sensitive did an automatic drawing of the event on the riverbank where Doli is supposed to have met his end. The gentleman's hand appeared to travel over the paper at tremendous speed as he sketched the scene. Naturally we remain a little sceptical about his analysis of our haunting.

Researchers have discovered that it is quite likely that our house is on a pilgrim route to St Winifred's Well at Holywell in Flintshire. The monks could have come from Shrewsbury or Valle Crucis Abbey in Llangollen. This ties in with some recent words on the wall: *pererindod* (pilgrimage) and *Amwythig* (Shrewsbury) with an arrow pointing towards *Treffynnon* (Holywell).

Providing Doli's haunting stays as friendly and benign as it is at present, he is a welcome part of our family.

Rose-Mary Gower, Mold, Flintshire, 1999

HELLO SAILOR

In the 1920s, in the East Park area of Wolverhampton, a young sailor by the name of Harry Parks Temple was drowned along with two young boys as he attempted to rescue them from a pool. He died a hero despite his failed rescue attempt.

Sometime in the late 1960s, my mother and her family were living in a terraced house in East Park. One night, while my mother and her older sister were talking before going to bed, they noticed a figure standing on the landing dressed in a sailor's uniform. They initially thought the figure to be their father, as he had served in the Navy during the war, but soon realised it was not. The sailor walked towards the bathroom and disappeared.

That was the only time that this particular figure was seen, although on subsequent occasions adult-sized hand prints and child-sized shoe prints appeared spontaneously on the walls and ceilings in different rooms of the house. These prints were painted over but mysteriously re-appeared and only disappeared when covered with wallpaper and ceiling tiles. I can recall actually seeing these prints on the walls of the front bedroom after the house was stripped when the remainder of the family moved out in the mid-Eighties. On another occasion, my mother's younger sister claims to have felt the presence of a young child brush past her in the hallway.

No contact has been made with the family that currently resides in the house to enquire whether the phenomena still occur, but I feel that Harry Parks Temple may still be making a rescue attempt which actually ended so tragically nearly 80 years ago.

Ian Deakin, Wolverhampton, West Midlands, 2000

SUICIDE SPECTRES

MURDEROUS GHOULS
Let me take you back some 30 years to a town in Malaysia, just across the border from Singapore. My father had just been promoted to the rank of Education Officer, and was entitled to free accommodation as a senior civil servant. The family was obviously delighted to occupy a large house and garden.

One evening during the first week after moving in, my elder brother, aged nine, appeared before us, totally speechless. All he could stutter was, "There... there... there's a skeleton hanging between the bedrooms." We eagerly went to investigate but found nothing amiss, and settled down to a quiet evening with my poor brother obviously distressed by the experience.

A few days later, I got up in the night to answer the call of nature. Though half-asleep, I made out the figure of a man standing in the dark by the doorway leading to my parents' bedroom. I assumed it was my dad and proceeded with my business. The next morning, I asked my dad what he was doing there the previous night. He said he had slept like a log and did not even hear me passing his room. This was followed by our live-in maid complaining that somebody kept shaking her up violently in the night.

A couple of weeks later, I came back from school at midday and was having my lunch alone when my younger brother, aged three, sitting on the stairs overlooking the dining room, cried, "Sis, who's that man sitting behind you?" Without looking back, I screamed and shouted for my mum, who emerged with a baton, convinced she had an intruder on her hands. But no one was to be seen. Over the next few weeks, things began to disappear without trace, including my braces which I had to wear to straighten my front teeth. We were all accused of carelessness. All victims of these mysterious 'thefts' were reprimanded by my dad, who seemed to be the only member of the household to escape these incidents.

Then mum suddenly fell violently ill. Doctors were called in as she drifted in and out of consciousness. She eventually pulled through, by which time dad had had enough. When he returned to work after mum had recovered, a colleague asked, "How's your wife?" Dad snapped back, "What the hell is wrong with this house?" With much arm-twisting, the man admitted that the house was believed to be haunted, with at least two men known to have taken their own lives there. One hanged himself at the spot where my elder brother allegedly saw a skel-

HIGH SPIRITS   IT HAPPENED TO ME!

> ## " *They claimed the ghosts had to take another life in order for them to rest in peace* "

eton. Another had poisoned himself.

By now, we were all so scared that we were going everywhere accompanied – even to the bathroom, where we would have the other person facing the wall! Dad consulted various religious bodies, who generally claimed that the ghosts had to take another life in order for them to rest in peace. Exorcists were hired; any signs of religion were removed in case of conflict in faith. Then my little brother fell seriously ill. My parents did not wait any longer: we moved out to temporary accommodation. Peace at last! Soon afterwards, we heard that the spirits had claimed a baby's life. Apparently the house has been exorcised several times now and is believed to be safe. But I, for one, am not going to find that out for myself.

Kayti Ooi, Milton Keynes, Bucks, 1994

GHOSTLY LADYKILLER

In 1944, when I was a child, my family had a big old house called Balgownie in Prestwick, near Ayr. The house had a 'presence' that walked up the stairs and into one of the bedrooms, which unfortunately happened to be the one where my elder brother Eion and I slept. It put the fear of God into us. Rex, the family dog, an enormous and extremely fierce animal, a cross between an Alsatian and a Labrador, was normally scared of nothing. Indeed, my mother kept him partly as a guard dog, as my father was away. However, whenever the presence walked he was terrified and became a trembling wreck and hid in my mother's bedroom.

At first she used to rush out to confront the intruder, dragging the terrified dog with her, then when the ghost walked straight past her, she would run into our bedroom and drag Eion and me out. Soon she moved us into another bedroom and the presence walked past the door of our room and into our old one through a closed door. I never actually saw the ghost, but the room became freezing cold and it was very creepy. Being a child, I just took it as a normal event. It was only later that I realised how strange it was.

After about a year, the Templetons, a local lawyer and his wife from nearby Ayr, came to live with us, to fill the house: otherwise, as it was wartime, strangers could have been billeted on us by the council. Mother gave them the ghost's room, but said nothing. A few weeks after they moved in, she took Eion and me to Glasgow to stay with relatives.

The very first night away, she had a phone call from Mrs Templeton who was in a terrible state. She was standing on the front doorstep with the phone on a long lead and refused to go back into the house. Her husband had made her go back inside and fetch the phone while he waited in the garden. As was its habit, the ghost had walked upstairs and into their bedroom through the closed door. They fled and refused to re-enter the house until mother returned. That night, they slept on the front door step. Shortly after this, my mother became ill and kept passing out for no apparent medical reason. Her condition grew worse and her doctor diagnosed appendicitis. They operated on her, but it made no difference and she became very ill; but still the hospital could find nothing wrong.

The war ended and she arranged the sale of the house and prepared to return to England. One day before we left, she was in the front garden when some neighbours passed by. They stopped and talked and she told them she was moving south. Then they told her that some 35 years earlier the owner of the house had committed suicide in the room where my brother and I had slept. His ghost was returning to the scene of the crime. He had apparently had marital trouble. Every woman who lived in the house after his death had become ill and died for no apparent reason. Their symptoms were all similar to my mother's.
Donald Crighton, Branksome Park, Dorset, 2004

THE CRYING GIRL
Late one evening at the boarding school where I teach a boy burst into the dormitory office looking pale and shaken. He managed to splutter something about the chapel and "the ghost". Somewhat taken aback, as this was a boy who normally displayed little emotion of any kind, let alone sudden expressions of childish nighttime fears, I told him to stop being foolish and go back to bed.

The first lesson any student learns on their incarceration here is of the broken-hearted girl who eternally walks the halls. A century ago, when these old buildings housed nuns and their young acolytes, the doomed girl was taken in against her will. Her parents had worried that she might forsake her honour with a certain local youth. Unable to cope, the poor child leapt from a vestry window and died.

"Please sir, just come and listen," the boy pleaded, nearly beside himself. Annoyed and not in the mood for such late-night foolishness, I followed him. Many boys were up, standing about in the corridor. Several huddled around the entrance to the chapel.

"For goodness sake!" I shouted. "Do you know what time it is? You're like a bunch of little girls!"

Someone nearly in tears said, "Sir, listen."

"To wha..."

Then I heard it. Faintly, but unmistakeably, from somewhere in the dark chapel, came singing. It was a girl's voice, sad, softly wailing. The sound was horribly moving. For a few moments I listened, utterly captivated. It took every shred of composure I had not to whimper like the children around me.

"Now listen boys," I said, hoping my voice didn't betray the fear I felt, "whatever is going on here has a rational explanation. Ghosts don't exist. I want you all to go back to your rooms please. I'll investigate this in the morning."

I did investigate it in the morning. For two years I've tried to find "a rational explanation". I have failed to do so.

Matthew Salt, Sidmouth, Devon, 2005

PHANTOMS OF WORLD WAR II

NAZI APPARITIONS

In 1992, as a private soldier serving in the Royal Army Medical Corps, I was transferred to a new unit, 1st Armoured Field Ambulance, based at Hohne in Germany. The unit was accommodated in Glynn Hughes Barracks, a former wartime German barracks quite imposing in appearance, with carved swastikas and other motifs still visible in the sandstone facing, despite numerous attempts to obliterate them by sandblasting. After each such attempt, everything would look smooth for a few months, and then the outline of the decorations would begin to return, as though indelibly imprinted on the 'spirit' of the building.

Also in the barracks was a wartime mortuary, used in the 1990s as an annex to the Quartermaster's Stores. Inside there remained a large marble slab, and one of the walls was decorated with a glorious Aryan warrior proclaiming it was "better to have died for the fatherland than lived a coward", or some such phrase.

The atmosphere within the camp was one of all-pervading gloom. Morale among the troops was low, and it was generally considered to be one of the worst postings you could get. Just prior to my arrival, a group of soldiers had been killed in a road accident, and during my (fortunately brief) stay, there was one accidental (not fatal) shooting, another fatal car crash, and an officer was killed when he fell from the roof of the nearby mess.

The site of Belsen concentration camp was a short walk away, and it was widely accepted that Glynn Hughes Barracks (named after the first medical officer to arrive at the liberated Belsen) had housed the camp's SS guards.

In such circumstances, it was hardly surprising that the place had a spine-tingling, spooky feel to it, but I was unaware of all this when I arrived from the UK. It turned out that I knew a couple of the lads from training, and was billeted in a room with one of them, a clerk known as "Indy". Sometime in the early hours of the morning, I was woken by shouting. I recognised the language as German, but at the time my linguistic skills were limited to ordering a beer and "Achtung! Spitfeur!" etc. I leapt out of bed, as the speaker appeared to be in the room, and

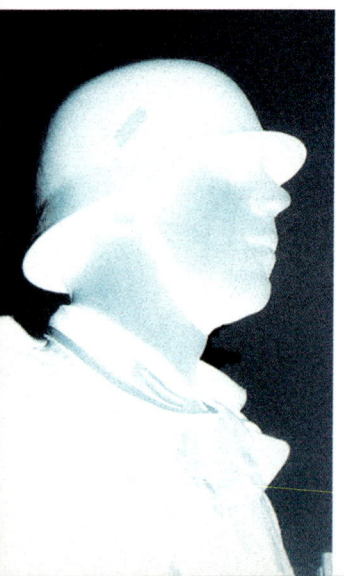

hit the light switch. Instant silence, and, predictably, no one in the room apart from myself and my sleeping roomie. It had seemed so real, but I chalked it up to dreaming, and went back to sleep. The next morning I mentioned my 'dream' to Indy, who replied, "Get used to it – we all get it..."

I don't know how, but I did get used to it. It became commonplace for newcomers in the unit bar, after a few drinks to loosen their tongues, to confess to hearing German voices during the night, or, less often but rather more chilling, the sound of children crying. Generally, it wasn't spoken about, and when it was, you could see the fear in the faces of those who had experienced it.

There were a couple of wagers on offer – to spend the night locked in the old mortuary carried a hefty reward of 1,000 DM, and up until the day the barracks was closed and returned to the German authorities no one ever claimed it. Dutch courage would lead to boasts of how a few were going to sit in the vast cellars beneath the camp and use a Ouija board, but again no one ever actually carried out the deed. At night, the camp sentries would sprint through the cellars on their rounds, not even stopping for an illicit cigarette.

Around six years later, while serving in Colchester, I was in conversation with an "old and bold" sergeant, and while listing previous units he mentioned he'd served in Hohne. I hadn't thought about the place in years, and had never related my experiences to anyone in the new unit. I asked him if anything strange had ever happened to him there. He told me that on his first night he'd been woken by voices and in the gloom had seen a figure wearing the distinctive German 'coal scuttle' helmet. He reached for the light switch and the figure vanished. It transpired that we'd both lived in the same room.
Neil Fielder-Mennell, Salisbury, Wiltshire, 2000

LINGERING GERMAN

One misty day in October 1952, when I was 11 years old and attending St George's Junior School in Notting Hill Gate, west London, my friend Jimmy and I bunked off in our dinner hour to explore the bomb site off Campden Hill Road. Of Tor Gardens only one shattered house remained, on a corner; the rest of the street had been totally flattened in the Blitz, along with large sections of Sheffield Terrace and Hornton Street. The area was a wasteland of rubble amidst bleak avenues of cadaverous, blackened houses. Rebuilding didn't get under way until late into the 1950s.

We entered that house in Tor Gardens and climbed a rickety flight of stairs that led directly into a room on the first floor. Leaning out of the window, I felt a strange sensation: everything seemed to have retreated into the distance, as if I had become incredibly small. This weird spatial distortion intensified until it became hardly bearable. I was on the verge of saying something about it to Jimmy when footsteps sounded on the stairs below, steadily approaching. We looked at each other, frozen with terror.

A man appeared in the doorway, aged about 25 with a fresh, clear face and cropped, blond hair. He was neatly dressed in a pale grey polo-necked sweater (rarely seen in the early 1950s), a light brown sports jacket, and dark grey trousers. In his right hand, firmly trained upon us, was a Luger pistol. I had seen Lugers in war comics and considered them a very stylish, superior-looking weapon.

"Vat are you doing here?" he enquired in a thick German accent. We were speechless as his eyes glared from one to the other of us.

"We're not doing anything," I finally blurted out, "We're just looking around."

"You should not be here. This is my house. You vill go now," he ordered, waving us towards the door with his gun.

We descended the stairs cautiously, not looking back, careful not to make any hasty moves that might invite a bullet, until, rounding the stairway on the ground floor, we legged it at full pelt back along Tor Gardens. At the corner of Campden Hill Road we paused to look at the upper window, but didn't see him.

My parents thought that Jimmy and I had been the victims of a prankster, who had patiently lain in wait for us just so he could go into his routine. Our friends, on the other hand, thought we had flushed out a German spy – a lone insurgent lurking in a ruined house plotting to overturn the Nazi defeat of seven years earlier.

Later, in my early twenties, a woman I knew mentioned, apropos of nothing, that she had moved into a block of flats in Tor Gardens. Neighbours had told her that the flats were haunted by the ghost of a young German who appeared on stair landings and in corridors, announced that he was lost, and then vanished without trace. The general theory was that this might be the ghost of a bomber pilot who had crashed onto Tor Gardens, his planeload of bombs creating the widespread devastation. I asked her about the location of the block where she lived, and it turned out to be on the corner of Tor Gardens and Hornton Street, where the lone bombed house had stood.

Malcolm Dickson, Derby, 2005

GHOSTS ON RECORD

BLOTTED OUT BY A BABY

Some years ago, a friend of my sister's moved into a new apartment. During the move, another friend took a Polaroid photo of the woman standing in her still-

" Perhaps it was the ghost of a bomber pilot who had crashed onto Tor Gardens "

empty living room, which photo eventually came into my sister's possession. I was told that it was at first perfectly normal, but that over the course of a week or two, the image of the woman was gradually overlaid with a close-up of a baby's face. By the time I saw the photo (some years after the event, I think), this had reduced the image of the woman to a vague outline in the background. I still get the shivers when I think about it.

That baby in the picture had a vaguely Victorian look about it, and I seem to recall that, though the original subject of the photo was in colour, the baby had a sepia tone. I certainly don't know of any way this photo could have been faked, and my sister isn't the type to make up spooky stories.
Peter Zolli, Worcester, Massachusetts, 1999

VEIL OF OBSCURITY

On 16 July 1994 I gave a reading at the Bridewell Theatre, a converted printers' institute in Bride Lane, off Fleet Street, London. The reading was part of a three-night 'Disobey' event arranged by Paul Smith of Blast First Records and writer Ian Sinclair, featuring Derek Raymond, Kathy Acker and Peter Whitehead.

My performance, scheduled for the last slot on Saturday night, was an attempt to combine poetry and ritual magic. The notion was to lead the audience through imaginary space by means of words and pre-taped ambient sound, starting with a stroll through the imaginary, mythical counterpart of the physical London that exists inside our minds and gradually moving on to less familiar mental spaces. Part of the verbal journey through the idea of London was a recounting of

IT HAPPENED TO ME! HIGH SPIRITS

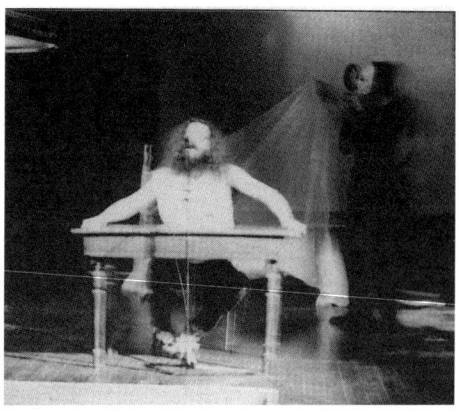

legend and history surrounding the building we were performing in and its environment, including St Bride's Church right next door to the theatre, where the first of Jack the Ripper's victims had been married in the 1860s.

Turning up on Saturday morning for a truncated rehearsal, I sat at the wooden table from which I would conduct the reading while my accomplice, David J, wearing a white mask, ran through some of the mimes he would be performing while I read. His prop during the rehearsal was a small, round mirror.

Seated in the front row and providing more or less our only audience for the run-through was my partner, comic artist Melinda Gebbie, who was taking snap shots. The picture above was among those returned from the lab.

Only myself and David J were on stage when the picture was taken. The hand visible behind David in the right background is not one of his, which are both raised to hold the mirror near his face. Neither was there any gauze or veil of any kind on stage at any time. The veil seems to be blowing outwards towards my seated figure from a point just behind David, extending over the right front corner of the table, where a stitched hem appears to be visible. Lower down, behind and to our right, there are a couple of horizontal stripes which, if interpreted as the layered hem of a Victorian skirt, would seem to suggest the figure of a woman, although it appears a lot less clear and substantial than the hand and veil.

After developing the pictures and lending me the sole print of this photograph, Melinda found that the packet containing the negatives had seemingly vanished from her house. I had a negative made from the existing print and ran off copies including the one you see here. Shortly after this, the packet of negatives turned up in a drawer at Melinda's house that had been searched thoroughly three times. The reappearance, however, did not include the original negative, which is still missing.

Alan Moore, The Twilight Zone, Northampton, 1995

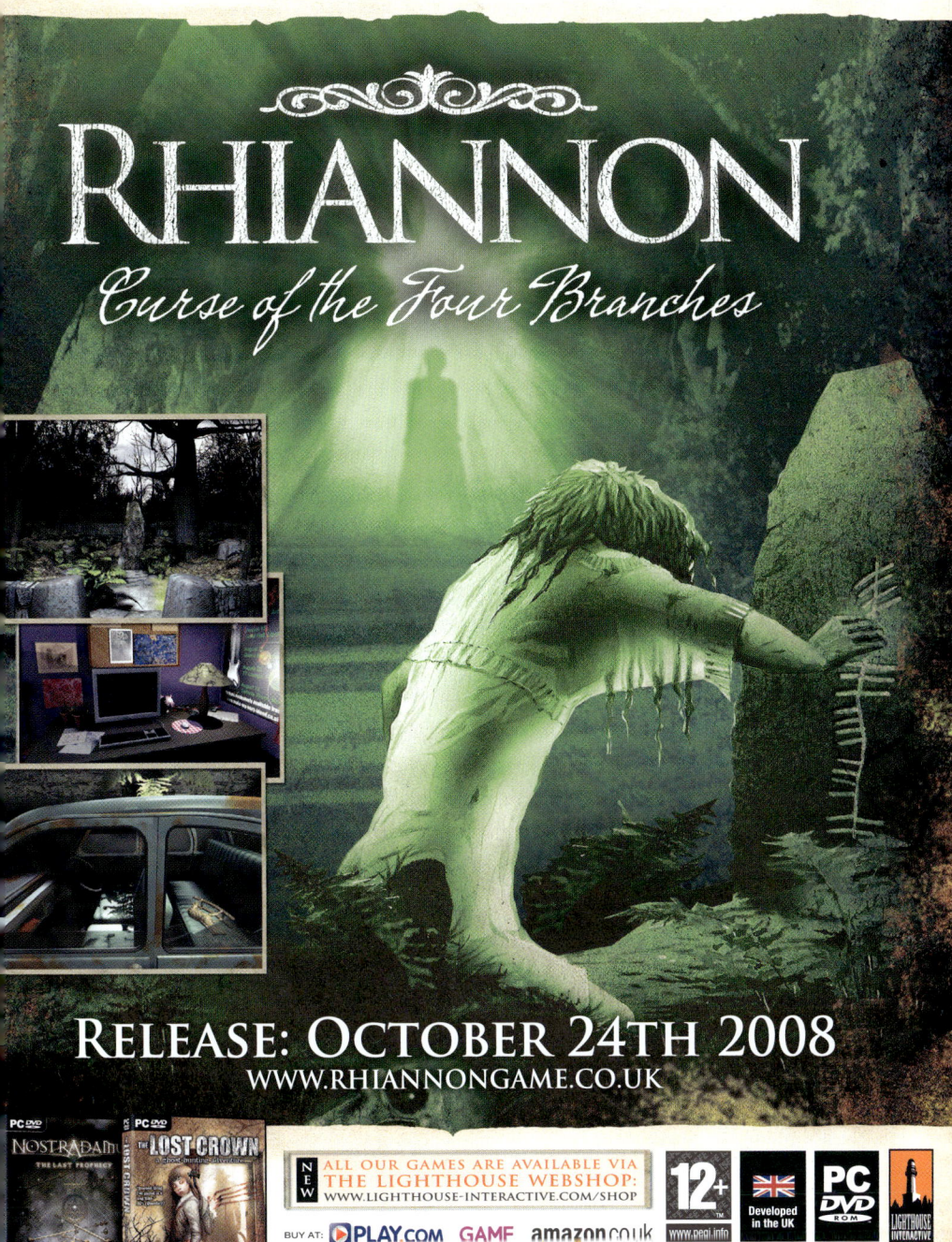

2 Don't Panic!

> A feeling of unease can escalate into incomprehensible terror for no apparent reason; the Ancient Greeks attributed such gut fear to the god Pan, and even today people occasionally sense the presence of the Cloven-hoofed One; others feel their dread relates to some past horror in the locality. Equally disturbing can be a temporary disorientation, making the familiar seem suddenly strange...

THE GREAT GOD PAN

ENCOUNTERING PAN

My first experience of a panic attack, which seemed extremely real to me, occurred at the age of 13. I was born into a working-class, Methodist family in Gateshead. It was a tightly regimented religious household and from an early age I was well acquainted with the Bible and especially the New Testament, though I knew nothing of ancient mythical deities.

I was very interested in biology, and liked nothing better than to go on excursions into the Northumberland countryside in my father's van. I was especially keen on roving round looking for new samples for my pressed flower collection.

On one such trip I wandered off into the empty, friendly countryside by myself, in search of collectable flowers while the rest of the family had a little picnic. I was on my own and enjoying myself, when I suddenly came upon a dead tree, in the branches of which sat a group of cawing crows. As I stood before it I was overwhelmed by a sense of dread, foreboding and evil, such as I had never experienced, even in the air-raid shelters of a few years previously. It was something I'd never felt in the countryside. I had to flee at once from this fearful place, and I was really terrified, though I heard no strange noises, except the cawing of the crows and the moan of the wind. I wanted to go straight home and my parents could not understand what was wrong with me.

In an English lesson with the long late Joe Howe, English master, for reasons I have forgotten, we touched on this subject. This was shortly afterwards and I was astonished when I heard him talk about this sense of terror that can befall people for no reason. I told him about my experience, which my parents would have considered some mental aberration. He looked at me intently and said, "Robinson, you have just encountered the ancient God Pan." I was rather taken aback by this statement, coming from an educated person, for as far as I knew educated persons were sensible and Christian. He then went on to use my experience as the basis of the derivation of the word 'panic'.

Many years later, as a student in Germany, I made a long *Wanderung* with a friend through the immense forests of Hessia, where we went for days without seeing anyone and, apart from the humming of the insects, I was aware of a kind of deep, background hum, that was not silence. My friend decided at one point to trick me by hiding in some trees, and this feeling returned, that what I was looking at, all the trees and bushes, was an illusion behind which lay something terribly powerful and hostile, that was somehow waiting for something, which seemed to be the elimination of man.

This powerful background awareness and this feeling of intense claustrophobia continued for half an hour, until I took to the expedient of throwing stones into the trees in an effort to make my friend reveal himself, which he did, when I hit the right spot. But that feeling of something deep, omnipresent, hostile and above all waiting remained with me, modified only by the return of his human presence and our reaching a remote and fairly undeveloped village, where we spent the night. I begged him never to do that again and, like my parents, he had no idea what I meant when I tried to explain this peculiar phenomenon.

I found this sinister feeling perfectly captured many years ago in a BBC TV Christmas broadcast of the MR James story 'The Three Crowns of Anglia', although there it was personalised and specific.
John Robinson, Ipswich, Suffolk, 2001

SOMEONE BEHIND YOU
In the spring of 1964, when I was 16, I was staying in a village in South Wales, at the home of Peter, a friend I had made the previous year. One evening, Peter suggested we try a wine glass séance. I was uneasy about this, having heard of

> **" *I felt it was head-and-shoulders taller than myself and walking on tip-toe...* "**

potentially harmful side-effects, but was not confident enough to say so. I would telephone my parents periodically when I was away from home, and I decided to make a call that evening. While Peter was setting the table for the séance, I walked the quarter mile alone to the telephone box in the village centre, as there was no phone in the house.

It was quite dark and the street lighting barely adequate, but I set off happily enough, rehearsing what I would say. After about 100 yards, I got that 'someone is behind you' feeling. I was slightly annoyed with myself for succumbing, but I couldn't resist turning round and looking. As expected, there was no one there and the feeling disappeared. I continued on my way. The sensation, when it almost immediately returned, was stronger, and it felt as though the mysterious entity was walking with its toes actually touching my heels and never losing contact as we walked. Again I turned, again the sensation disappeared, again it returned, almost immediately, as I continued.

This time, the impression had taken on another dimension. I felt it was head-and-shoulders taller than myself and was walking on tip-toe! What on earth was going on? Was this the Devil? Had all this talk of séances conjured some entity? I looked again, turning full circle this time. Nothing! I felt decidedly uncomfortable as I continued walking. I was getting near the village centre by this time; surely if this was a creature of darkness it would be disturbed by the brighter light of the shopping area, and would leave me alone.

As I neared the friendly neon of the shops, my perception of the entity increased as it seemed to manifest ever more strongly. It was towering over me, even though I was already near my adult height of over six feet. It was, as before, walking on tip-toe and literally on my heels and I became aware that it was laughing at me – not a malicious laugh, but a teasing, playful, mischevious laugh. I knew then that whatever or whoever it was meant me no harm.

I tried something I had read about in a book on the paranormal. I turned around and, while concentrating on trying to project caring, loving thoughts, said quietly and carefully: "Are you a troubled spirit, can I help you?" I hadn't the faintest idea what I would do if it said "Yes", but the problem didn't arise. As I finished speaking, I got the impression of absolute amazement, followed by the sensation of the entity moving away from me at enormous speed somewhere to my right front. The feeling was exactly like that cartoon image of Wile E. Coyote falling into a canyon and becoming, within a second or so, a vanishing pinpoint. When I continued on my way, the sensation had gone, and never returned.

I made my telephone call and returned to tell my tale, but nobody was particularly interested. During the séance, we apparently contacted a Roman centurion. Peter asked him how he died and the glass moved rapidly and apparently randomly, whereupon I broke contact by removing my finger. I felt we had gone far enough.

Many years later, during the 1970s, I came upon a book about the Findhorn Foundation containing a lucid account of a meeting with Pan on Edinburgh's Princes Street. The description of Pan, whom I'd always thought to be quite small, was intriguing. Half man, half goat, some seven and a half feet tall, and walking with apparent ease on the tips of his hooves, he has a wonderfully warm, jovial, bubbling personality that constantly bursts out in shouts of laughter. No one but the narrator saw him, and they walked up and down Princes Street with Pan's arm round the shoulders of his human companion. For myself, I was left wondering about that night in Wales.

After seeing Michael Bentine's one-man show, 'From the Ridiculous to the Paranormal' in September 1992, I wrote him an account of my strange experience, and he phoned me to talk about it. He said I had encountered a Pan archetype. Such meetings, he said, are a rare event and not always pleasant. People who had been cruel to animals, in particular, meet a fearsome and vengeful entity. He then, unprompted, endorsed my own belief that I would have another visit. I await that meeting with interest!

John D Ritchie, Doncaster, South Yorkshire, 1993

THE NOONDAY DEVIL

At about the age of 50, I was walking alone in the open countryside near Fiesole, north of Florence, around noon, when I was seized with utter panic. I had been thinking how this scene was the result of thousands of years of cultivation. It was not particularly wild, indeed very close to the small town. Yet I had the strongest sensation of not being *wanted* by some local force, half-god, half-human, and this intense disquiet persisted until I had got some distance away from the spot.

Years later, I read how EM Foster had had an identical experience at very much the same place. I am a surgeon and well aware that one must be careful about such experiences. If they occur at midday, before lunch, it may be due to a low blood-sugar. It may be the *accidie*, or noonday devil, of depression and isolation described by the ancients. One may just be neurotic. But this was none of these, it was an experience of *place*, and I have never had it again or anywhere else.
David Le Vay, Burwash, East Sussex, 2001

THE FACE OF PAN

I've followed the accounts of various panic attacks with huge interest. A similar thing happened to me in the lower Rhondda Fawr valley, in what was then Glamorgan, now Rhondda Cynon Taff. A steep lane starts opposite and slightly south of the entrance to Dinas Mines Rescue Station. It has deteriorated and is no longer driveable. Follow this uphill for about 200 yards. At the end of the lane – beware ferocious geese – look left and you will see the remains of a small quarry, long abandoned.

About 1961, when I was about nine, I looked at the quarry, which was much less overgrown with ivy than it is now. Within seconds it had turned into a face, with a long, straight nose, a 'Judge Dredd' style chin, and an evil, knowing grin. Its forehead was tall and rather square. It was wearing a sort of small crown or coronet. The face didn't move, but the eyes, small and bright blue, swivelled around to look at me. I was absolutely certain that the look from the eyes was intended to kill me. I ran home, a distance of about one mile, spun my mother some yarn about being chased by a wasp, and huddled in bed for the rest of the day in a state of terror. I've never told the truth of the matter to anyone until now.

I recovered after a few weeks, and together with my best friends of the time, a pair of identical twins, I often revisited the site. Nothing like an appearance of Pan ever happened to me again, but strange things turned up there, for instance: a pile of ampoules, most shattered, but some containing a clear liquid. Next, hundreds, possibly thousands, of primitive, crudely moulded tin soldiers, all printed with four eyes. Then a large pile of soot. We found numerous other odd things there, but after 40 years I can't remember them. Whenever we found anything new, we always noticed that the previous stuff had been cleared away, with not the slightest trace remaining.

Tragically, about two years later, a boy aged about 14 was found there, dead. I knew him: we were in school together. I don't think any credible cause of death was ever found. Could he have been frightened to death?
Viv Hobbs, Blackwood, Gwent, 2001

THE LIVING DAYLIGHTS

ST PAUL'S REVENGE

My husband Alan and I lived in Istanbul for a time and because we had our own transport we managed some wonderful touring holidays. One very hot day at the ruined city of Ephesus, we climbed up the theatre terraces. Half way up we sat down to view the ancient surroundings. After a while Alan said he would like to walk up to the top of the theatre to take some photographs. I was left sitting there just looking around. I was thinking what a lovely splash of colour the T-shirts on a group of tourists made against the grey stone architecture when suddenly I was filled with so much fear and panic I could hardly breathe. I rushed up to my husband at the top of the theatre.

"Whatever is the matter?" Alan asked, showing great concern. "I don't know," I replied. "I'm just very, very frightened." The next question he asked was: "Where is my wallet and your bag?" I had left them where I had been sitting. He collected them as I didn't want to return anywhere near that place.

What had caused that extreme fear? Some of our friends laughed when we told them, and said, "Well, you have often argued strongly about some of St Paul's teachings, perhaps he was getting his own back." The thing is, I actually hadn't thought about St Paul when I was at Ephesus. We have a photograph Alan took of me rushing up the theatre, before he knew I was so frightened. I never had such an attack before or since.
Joy Ferguson, Derby, 2001

FEAR IN THE FURS

About 40 years ago, when I was eight, I went blackberrying with my mother and our dog Rachel at a place called the Furs, between Chieveley and Peasemore in Berkshire. Suddenly I said to my mother, "Let's go home," and she said, "Yes child, let's hurry." Half a mile down the road, I noticed that Rachel wasn't with us, but my mother said she would make her own way back.

When we got home, my grandmother asked what we had done to Rachel. The dog had arrived home 15 minutes before us in an agitated state and hid for several hours behind a curtain under the sink. Neither I nor my mother had seen or heard anything at the Furs, although others had reported humming and nearby there was supposed to be a Viking burial ground. We didn't talk about it outside the family, and to think of it now makes the hair on the back of my neck stand up.
Mary Behrens, Layton, Utah, 2001

NAMELESS DREAD

The following occurred in 1977 in an area of the countryside over which, in July 1644, the battle of Marston Moor was fought. I was then a postgraduate student working on my D.Phil thesis, and as a form of light relief from the work, had begun in 1974 a secondary research project on the battlefield, intending by study of the terrain to try and interpret the conflicting documentary evidence. I had liberty to wander wherever I wished, and in all seasons of the year and all weathers, over a large tract of land in which it was rare to encounter anyone

DON'T PANIC! IT HAPPENED TO ME!

> **"Suddenly, I was filled with so much fear and panic that I could hardly breathe"**

else. I was usually alone, and quite content.

It was a summer afternoon, a little overcast, and I was walking (for the thousandth time) up what is known as Sugar Hill Lane away from a place called Four Lanes Meet, quite some distance from any roads. Sugar Hill Lane was, and still is, a wide drove road fringed with tall oaks, with a particular peaceful charm. In a field to my left, a number of bullocks were grazing. I became aware quite suddenly of their agitation, which showed itself in a desperate milling around, those on the outside of what was effectively a circle of beasts, striving to get inside and making a fearful racket about it. As suddenly as it began, it stopped, and I walked on for a little way only to be overcome by a powerful desire to go no further.

This was not a panic, yet: merely a sense of change in the atmosphere of the lane. I turned, and walked back, frequently glancing behind and to the side of me, until within 50 yards of Four Lanes Meet, I very reluctantly broke into a spurt, and only stopped running when I had passed into a wide, hedgeless field of standing wheat. I was annoyed with myself, and stayed a long time looking back along the lane. A day or so later I made myself walk its length again, but experienced nothing unusual.

This episode has been unique in my life, and I am a great favourer of remote, unpeopled places. It remains vivid to me all these years on; it was as if something had intruded into the landscape with which I merely happened to coincide.

Dr P Young, York, 2001

SPOOKED IN THE HIGHLANDS
In the early 1980s, a friend and I, on holiday in Scotland near Aviemore, decided to take her small dog for an hour's walk in a forested area near the guesthouse where we were staying. It was a late afternoon or early evening at the end of June, fine weather, so the light was still very good.

We started to walk along the forest track, and after about 10 minutes came to a clearing where the road forked. There was an old-fashioned caravan (the type that roadmen would have used before World War II) parked in the clearing, but no sign of any activity. At the edge of the clearing we both stopped and said: "Which way?" Then, together, one of us said: "I don't want to go any further," and the other said: "Let's turn back." My friend said: "It's spooky, isn't it?" and I thoroughly agreed. We couldn't get away from the spot quickly enough, and on comparing notes afterwards we discovered that both of us had the hair on the back of our necks standing up.

When we reached the road again, we were puzzled to find that the gate that we had struggled to open to gain access to the forest and had given up on and squeezed in round the side, was mysteriously lying wide open. Who had been there in that 15 minutes, miles out in the countryside, and opened the gate?

When we arrived back at the guesthouse, we related the events to the owner, who promised to make enquiries about the forested area. My friend returned with her husband to the guesthouse the following year, and was told there was a cottage down the lane we had walked down. This had been standing derelict for many years, and had been bought and modernised, but the new owners had lived in it for only a fortnight before departing. The cottage had not been lived in again after that.
Mrs E Knight, Norley, Cheshire, 2001

FLEEING THE WENDIGO
I was living in central Canada in 2000 and was off work for about two months due to a sports injury. During my rehabilitation, I did a lot of hiking and small game hunting on the outskirts of the city. One afternoon, I found myself a little deeper into the forest than I intended, and decided to head back – my leg had not fully healed, and I became aware of how lonely it was out there. As I walked, the sun seemed to go down quicker than I had expected. The calibre of rifle was only capable of killing small game, and there were native stories in the area concerning a spirit or creature called the Wendigo. I was fighting off

mild panic when I heard a sound that I have never heard before or since, and it turned my blood cold. It sounded like a human growling, but with echoes of children growling or screaming in unison. The image I got in my head was of an attack of huge flies or piranhas or something. The sound emanated from the top of a forested hill off to my right, about 75ft (23m) away. I couldn't have been more scared if someone had a gun to my head.

I made it back to my truck about five minutes later, jumped into the cab and put my head down on the steering wheel as I exhaled deeply. Safety. I waited there for maybe a minute before I put the key in the ignition. At the same time, some dirt or sand was thrown at the side window, and something smashed into the back of the truck hard enough to knock the tools around in the back. Needless to say, I didn't stick around to shake its hand. Although I have no trouble going into dense forest during the day, I still have bad dreams and slight anxiety I attribute to this incident.

LU, by email, 2002

SUDDENLY LOST

PIXIE-LED

I have worked as a teacher in the same school for the past 12 years and commute 25 miles (40km) each way every day. In 1998 I was returning home at around 10pm after an evening commitment, along country lanes which I have travelled twice a day all year round, when I found that I didn't recognise a single feature. I dropped my speed, opened the window and turned up the radio, and still had no idea where I was. Being an advocate of the Dirk Gently method of navigation I drove on at 30mph (48km/h) for five or six miles... and suddenly everything dropped into place. This has never happened before or since, thank goodness, but the feeling of helplessness has stayed with me very strongly.

While watching the television programme 'Meet the Ancestors' I realised that the Tormarton bodies (iron age skeletons) were found yards from the road where the incident occurred, an area also rich in hill forts. Could there be some 'sacred geometry' at work here creating confusion for the innocent?

Graham Hill, by email, 2001

IT HAPPENED TO ME! **DON'T PANIC!**

JAMAIS VU
One day in mid-July 2001, I was in a pub in the Southover area of Brighton, East Sussex, waiting for a friend to appear for a drink. At 8.12pm she telephoned to say she was in Queens Park and on her way. This park is about 10 minutes away from the pub I was sitting in. At 8.29 she called again to say she was lost in the park and couldn't find her way out, but I was to wait for her and she would arrive as soon as she could. Very distressed, she finally arrived at the pub at 8.45. The peculiar thing is that Queens Park is approximately a quarter of a mile (400m) long and an eighth of a mile (200m) wide and has at its north end a pink tower visible from most of the park. As it was still daylight we cannot account for this strange loss of bearings.
Tony Baldwin, by email, 2001

LOST IN BRIGHTON
Tony Baldwin may be interested to know of similar cases of disorientation in Brighton when I lived and worked there in the 1970s. For about an hour in broad daylight, I experienced a very disturbing sense of not being able to find my way out of some streets in the Preston Park area, an area I know well. I have never found an explanation, nor have I had the sensation before or since. On another occasion, a client phoned my office in the Clock Tower area saying she was lost. She was in a phone box within direct sight of my offices, a place she knew well. She also could offer no explanation.
Rod York, Worcester, 2001

MIND FOG
One day in 2000, I had just collected an item I had ordered and was passing through the Mander Centre, Wolverhampton, on my way home. The Centre has four exits, which I know very well, but on trying to reach the exit I wanted I was perplexed and not a little frustrated to find that no matter how hard I tried, I always ended up at the wrong one. This state of affairs lasted for around 15 minutes with me wandering round in circles before the spell was broken and I was able to locate the exit I desired.
Anthony Smith, Bilston, West Midlands, 2002

Telescope Planet

0844 804 0060
www.telescopeplanet.co.uk
Telescope Planet, 8 Mansel Street, Swansea, SA1 5SF

Telescopes • Binoculars • Cameras Spotting Scopes • Microscopes Monoculars • Tripods
Night vision • Astronomy Books • Software • Solar Observing • Astrophotography

Celestron Astromaster
Dual purpose telescope for terrestrial and celestial viewing. Produces bright, clear images of the Moon and planets.

AZ	£74
EQ	£94
114 EQ	£115
130 EQ	£125
EQ	£139
AZ	£139
130 EQ+motor	£165
EQ+motor	£169

Perfect starter 'scope!

Celestron NexStar SE
- Maksutov-Cassegrain telescope
- Combines the classic heritage of the original tube telescopes with the latest state-of-the-art features
- StarBright XLT high transmission coatings come standard
- StarPointer finderscope to help with alignment and accurately locating objects
- Internal flip mirror
- Quick release fork arm mount, no-tool setup
- Sturdy computerized altazimuth mount
- Internal battery compartment
- Ultra sturdy steel tripod features built-in wedge
- Includes CD-ROM "The Sky" Astronomy Software

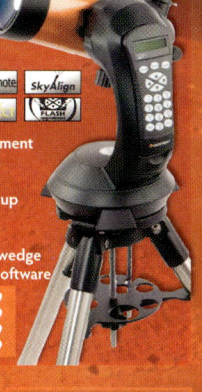

Nexstar 4SE	£339
Nexstar 5SE	£589
Nexstar 6SE	£739
NexStar 8SE	£1059

NexImage
NexImage CCD £105

Celestron NexImage Solar System CCD. View and capture live video on your computer screen. Quick start instructions, tutorial, and sample video file.

TP 50mm refractor
A great scope to start out with. Extremely light, ideal for very young children. Perfect for viewing the stars and Moon with ease.

Includes:
50mm Refractor Telescope
Tripod
2 Eyepieces
Barlow Lens
Manual
Star Diagonal

TP 50mm refractor £29

TP 70mm refractor
Perfect starter scope, reduced for limited time. This new telescope/spotter is perfect for daytime nature viewing. Ideal to sit on your table. Comes with 70mm telescope tube
2 x Eyepieces
Barlow Lens
Erecting Eyepiece
Tripod

TP 70mm refractor . £29.99

TP 60mm refractor Pkg
This Scope now comes in Black. Everything you could think of in one Package.

60mm Refractor Telescope
3 Eyepieces, viewfinder barlow lens, accessory tray, tripod, hard carry case, free delivery

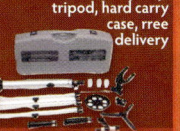

TP 60mm refractor £49

Bresser Sirius
A high quality 70mm refracting telescope with excellent optics and a full-sized 31.7mm (1.25") eyepiece diameter. Fine adjustment mechanism on the alt-az mount. With three eyepieces and a Barlow lens. Six magnification powers

Bresser Sirius 60mm ... £69

SkyWatcher Infinity-76 3"
Mag: x30
Primary Mirror: 76mm
Focal Length: 300mm (f/4)
Eyepiece Supplied: x30
Erecting (*suitable for terrestrial use)
Parabolic Primary Mirror
Helical Focusing
Complete with Neckstrap
Table-Top Cradle
Gift Box

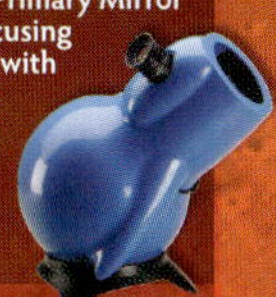

Infinity £39.99

Skywatcher-130P Explorer SupaTrak
130mm motorised parabolic reflector auto-tracking scope.
500mm focal length. 650mm focal length, red dot finder, 2 eyepieces, tripod and accessory tray.

Explorer-130P SpTrak .£199

Books
We carry a massive range of astronomy books including all of the Philips range. Just call to make an order.

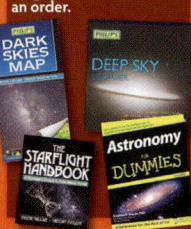

Starry Night Software

FREE online upgrade to V6.3

Starry Night	£29.99
New Starry Night Enthusiast V6	£49.99
Starry Night Pro V6	£99.99
Starry Night Pro Plus V6	£149.99

New MySky Plus
Just point and shoot to identify planets, stars, constellations. See images, watch video and hear audio descriptions. Take guided tours of the night sky. Simple controls, easy to use. Free connection cable

Meade MySky £299

Skyscout Planetarium

SkyScout	£249
"All about stars" expansion card	£14
"Astronomy for beginners" expansion card	£14
SkyScout Scope	£159
SkyScout speaker	£20
Connect controller	£79

Customer Service and sales: **0844 804 0060** local rate
Tracking numbers, sales and advice: **01792 475 744**
Technical advice, sales (showroom): **01792 475 745**

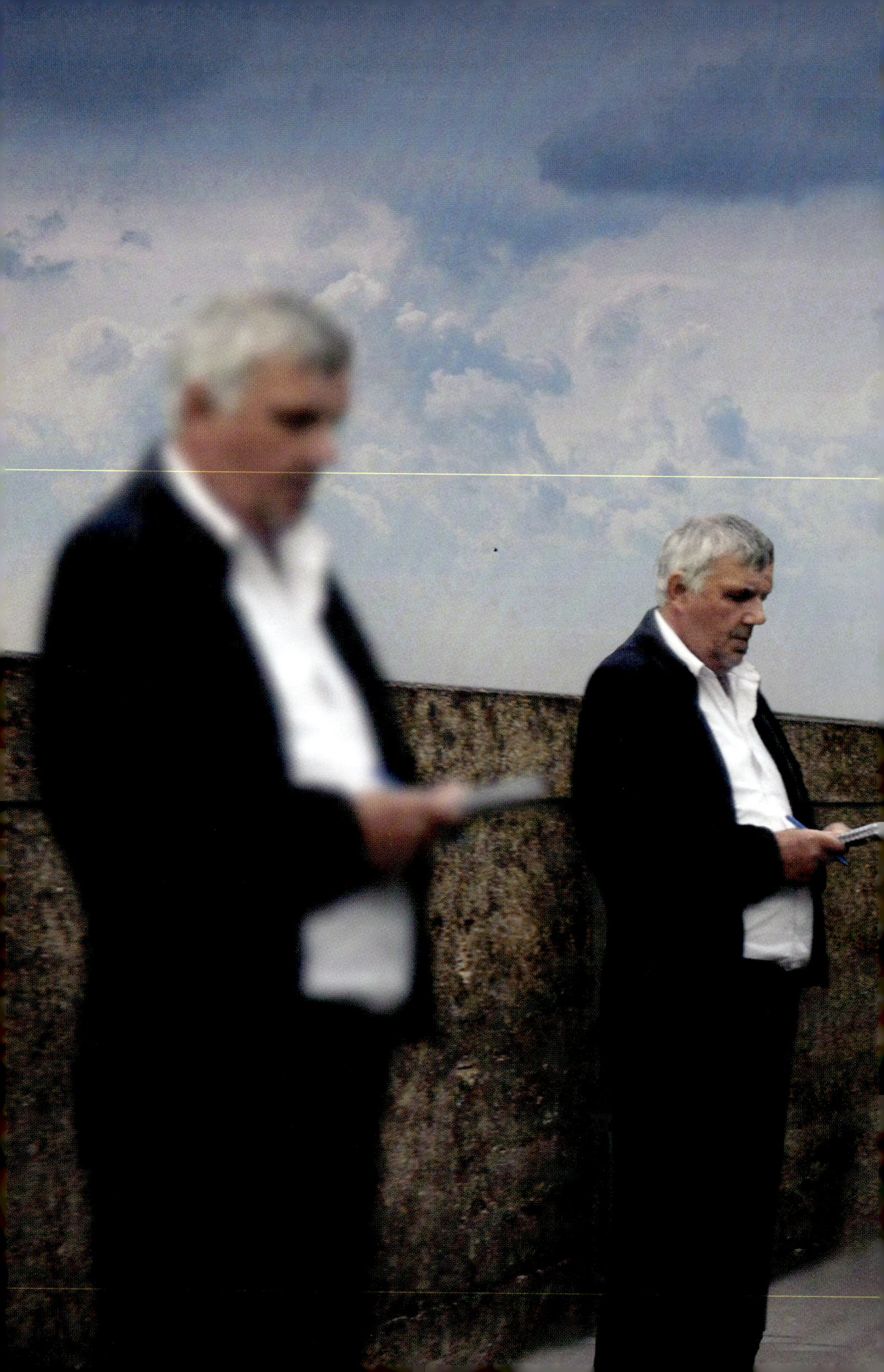

3 Double Trouble

> We assume that we are unique, but occasionally we appear to be in two places at once, like those saints who reputedly had the gift of bilocation; but maybe some of us have actual doubles – or doppelgängers – acting under their own volition. A related phenomenon is the look-alike who heralds our arrival: this is the vorgänger, known in Iceland as the *Fylgia* and in Norway as the *Vardogr*.

DOPPELGÄNGERS

THEY DWELL AMONG US

In the summer of 1980, I started seeing a strange little guy at the bus stop in Calgary on weekday mornings. His skin, eyes and hair all looked artificial. He had a grey suit and briefcase for that "totally normal" look, and always stared at the paper. He never made a sound, never looked up, his eyes never scanned the page or blinked, he never turned the page. He got on the bus with me and stayed on till after my stop. I kept thinking he looked just like something disguised as a human being.

    This went on exactly the same every day for a few days. Then one day he wasn't there, but he got on at the next stop round the corner – so I figured he was running late and would've missed the earlier stop, and probably lived close to both of them. Next day he was back at my stop again, got on with me, and then at the next stop round the corner, another guy got on who looked exactly, and I mean *exactly*, like him. They both stared at their papers, neither one acknowledging the other's presence in any way. No one else on the bus appeared to notice that there were two absolutely identical guys on board with them. It was as if I was the only one who could see, or the only one who wasn't in on it. That was my last day living in that neighbourhood so I never saw either of them again.
John MacLeod, Canada, 2003

IT HAPPENED TO ME! DOUBLE TROUBLE

MAKE MINE A DOUBLE
Last week, our small and already slightly odd town of Tiverton had widely reported sightings of UFOs. A couple of days later, a colleague at work asked me where I had been off to the previous evening, as she had seen me riding in the opposite direction to my usual route home. She was certain it was me: same coloured crash helmet, same jacket and *exactly* the same motorcycle. This is very unlikely, as my motorbike is a 20-year-old Kawasaki with a very distinctive green and silver colouring and murals on the side panels. There are no other 20-year-old GPZ550s in my area, let alone customised ones. So who was this other me with the same bike gear, the same bike, and the same very long red hair?

If that wasn't odd enough, the next day, my colleague's very own doppelgänger was seen in the town at 8.30am, when she was 16 miles (26km) away at a meeting in Exeter. It was convincing enough to cause quite an argument in the office between her and another member of staff who insisted he had seen her walking along the high street an hour before.
Kes Cross, Tiverton, Devon, 2004

THAILAND TWIN
I studied travel industry management at a small US mountain college from 1990 to 1995. There was an exchange programme with a university in Thailand, and in my last year of study I went to Chiang Mai in northern Thailand for a resort internship and then spent another week with a friend in Bangkok. Since returning from Thailand, I lost contact with many of my former friends until recently.

I received an indignant email a few months ago from my friend in Bangkok asking me why I hadn't informed him that I was visiting his city. He said he was stuck in a traffic jam on Sukhumvit Road – Bangkok's most important road – when I had walked directly beside his car a few feet from him, which afforded him a face-to-face, close-up view. He rolled down his window and waved and spoke to me but I was totally unresponsive and kept walking.

This was someone whom I knew very well over a period of many years and he would easily recognise my Anglo-Welsh face anywhere, but especially amongst a crowd of Thais where I would have stood out. My doppelgänger was dressed in my manner, had the same type of haircut and mannerisms, and my distinctive walk. I emailed him back assuring him that I was in the USA at the time of this sighting and had not been anywhere near Bangkok for over eight years; but to this day he insists that it was, in his words, "a hundred per cent you".

> " *He said we had served in Vietnam together... but I was never in the Army* "

This is only the most recent example of my doppelgänger making an appearance. About two years ago I was having blood drawn for routine medical tests when the attending nurses welcomed me back into the laboratory and asked me to please be more co-operative this time while being stuck with a syringe. I asked what they meant. It seems that I had been in just a bit earlier that same morning and had put up quite a fight while having my blood drawn, which is totally out of character for me. The nurses both insisted that not only did the earlier patient look and talk exactly like me but had on the exact same clothes as I was wearing. I assured them that it wasn't me because I was in my GP's office during that time; to which they replied that I must then have an identical twin in town who shopped in the same clothing stores as I did.
Alex Jones, Chapel Hill, North Carolina, 2003

BROTHERS IN ARMS
In 1982 I lived on the east side of Milwaukee, Wisconsin. At a grocery store I frequented, a man unknown to me said: "Hi Dave". I passed it off as insignificant. Two months later, the same thing happened in the parking lot of the store. Questioned, he replied that we had served in Vietnam together and that my hometown was Two Rivers, Wisconsin. I actually grew up in Manitowoc, five miles (8km) away. The visual resemblance, same first name and proximity of birthplaces was interesting. But I was never in the Army or in Vietnam.

I forgot about the incident until 1992, when I stopped at a tavern 20 miles (32km) from the east side of Milwaukee. There was a couple sitting close by who

IT HAPPENED TO ME! DOUBLE TROUBLE

kept staring at me and I had no idea why. When the man went to the restroom, the woman said: "Aren't you going to say hello, Dave?"

In the ensuing conversation I found out I served in the same platoon in Vietnam as her husband and was a good friend. Their Dave had gone to the University of Wisconsin-Milwaukee at the same time that I was enrolled, and had lived five blocks from where I had my apartment. In combat, you know the people around you. I am at a loss to explain how a person with the same name, the same physical characteristics (down to my moustache and eyes), grows up five miles away from me, goes to the same college, lives so close to me and is recognised by strangers decades later.

David Zanotti, Milwaukee, Wisconsin, 1997

TWO-WAY MIRROR

One afternoon in July 1980, during my visit to London, I went to Bond Street to look at antique shops. In a quiet lane I saw an elderly woman taking a nap against a wall with a wide-brimmed hat shading her face. There was a small cart of second-hand books by her side. As I passed, she looked up and I saw that she resembled my mother exactly.

I asked for directions to a particular shop. "Stay here please," she said, gazing at me. "I'll see if it's open." She disappeared round the corner and moments later returned to tell me that it was.

"Why are you so kind to me?" I asked, giving her my thanks.

"Well," she answered smiling, "because you look exactly like my son Jeff." She pulled out a photo of him from her purse. It was a good likeness of me, though a bit younger. He had on a check shirt, exactly like the one I had some years ago!

Cyrus Ganjavi, Tonekabon, Mazandaran, Iran, 1999

BILOCATION

SEEING IS DISBELIEVING

"What on earth happened to you after we parted last night?" a friend asked me one morning recently.

I stared at her. "Nothing. Why?"

"You didn't catch your bus home – but I saw you getting on it!"

Indeed she had; after our evening class we'd chatted at the town terminus as usual until my bus arrived, then I got aboard and she went towards her house a couple of minutes' walk away. "Yes, of course I caught it." And had been unusually thankful to reach home; I was recovering from flu and felt very tired after the evening's exertions.

"But you turned around and came back into town? You must have." She wasn't joking.

"Certainly not. Once I reached home I stayed there. Yvonne, what's all this about?" I added – lightly, teasing – "Don't tell me I've got a double."

Then the story came out. Her daughter Nicola had come home half an hour after she did and slightly more than half an hour after my bus left. Yet Nicola – a level-headed woman in her twenties, who knows me well – claimed, and could not be budged from her statement, that she had seen me waiting at the bus terminus two minutes before. She described my appearance and clothes in detail and without error (curly fair hair, white raincoat, brown shoes, glasses). I had spoken to her, had said, "Hello Nicky," and she and I had talked for several minutes; she recognised my face, as well as my voice and American accent. Nicola became angrily insistent when her mother doubted all this, so Yvonne decided some emergency must have brought me back into town. She hurried round the corner to the bus terminus but, although no buses had arrived or left since Nicola passed by, no one was waiting. The night was cold and silent, the surrounding streets deserted.

All three of us are in sound health, mental as well as physical. Nicola has excellent eyesight; she is now as baffled and perplexed over the incident as are her mother and myself. The clothes I wore that night are ones I seldom wear; she would not automatically associate them with me and could not have seen me or them earlier that evening.

So what is the explanation? I was, as I said, unusually tired and felt almost light-headed with fatigue by the time I reached home, but Yvonne did see me board the bus and I did travel home on it and stay there; confirmation of this is available from other sources. Moreover, although tired, I was definitely aware of what I was doing. The fact is that when Nicola saw what she took to be me at the bus terminus and we chatted, my body was not there; nor, apparently, was any living person who closely resembled me (assuming so exact a likeness were credible in this small town and that her knowledge of what I wore that evening could somehow be explained away).

IT HAPPENED TO ME! DOUBLE TROUBLE

"Any living person" – there's the rub. A friend of mine in another town recently had a similar experience: four of her colleagues at work saw her arrive at the office half an hour before she actually did arrive, and again she can prove that she was not there when they saw her. Neither she nor I had any previous belief or interest in ghosts, spirit bodies or other psychic phenomena. She, like myself, was unusually tired and under some stress at the time of the occurrence.

Since then I have read some of the literature about doppelgängers, spirit-doubles of the living. I would be glad to find a solid scientific explanation, but none presents itself. My nerves stir in an unfamiliar way when I think of what happened.

Patricia Tyrrell, Newquay, Cornwall, 1994

FANCY MEETING YOU

Last year my husband died unexpectedly at the age of 32 and as a result I have had a lot of trouble getting to sleep at night, not managing to drop off until 4 or 5am. One particular night last December, lying in bed still fully awake, I turned over to see what the time was and found myself face to face with myself! There I was standing beside the bed. I childishly hid my head under the duvet hoping my (other) self would disappear, but when I dared to turn down the cover there "I" still stood, dressed in my coat and hat, gazing down at "me" in my pyjamas. Unfortunately, I was distracted by my youngest son crying. I turned to check on him (he sleeps in bed next to me) and when I looked back "I" had gone!

Deborah Cameron, Blackpool, 1995

FRIEND DUPLICATED

In the autumn of 1996, my flatmate and I invited a mutual friend over for dinner. The evening was going well, and we decided to visit a local bar. Our flat lay at the far end of a terraced cul-de-sac, so we had to walk nearly its full length to reach the main road – North Hill, in central Plymouth. I remember it as being a still, clear night. It was pretty dark, but the street lamps meant we were able to see clearly up and down the length of the pavement. As we lived in a dead end, there was no through traffic, and the pavement was deserted as usual.

We had just started down the street, when my flatmate realised he'd forgotten something and rushed back to get it. My friend and I waited where we were standing and carried on chatting. After a few minutes, I heard our front door slam, then as my flat mate caught up with us, we moved apart slightly to make

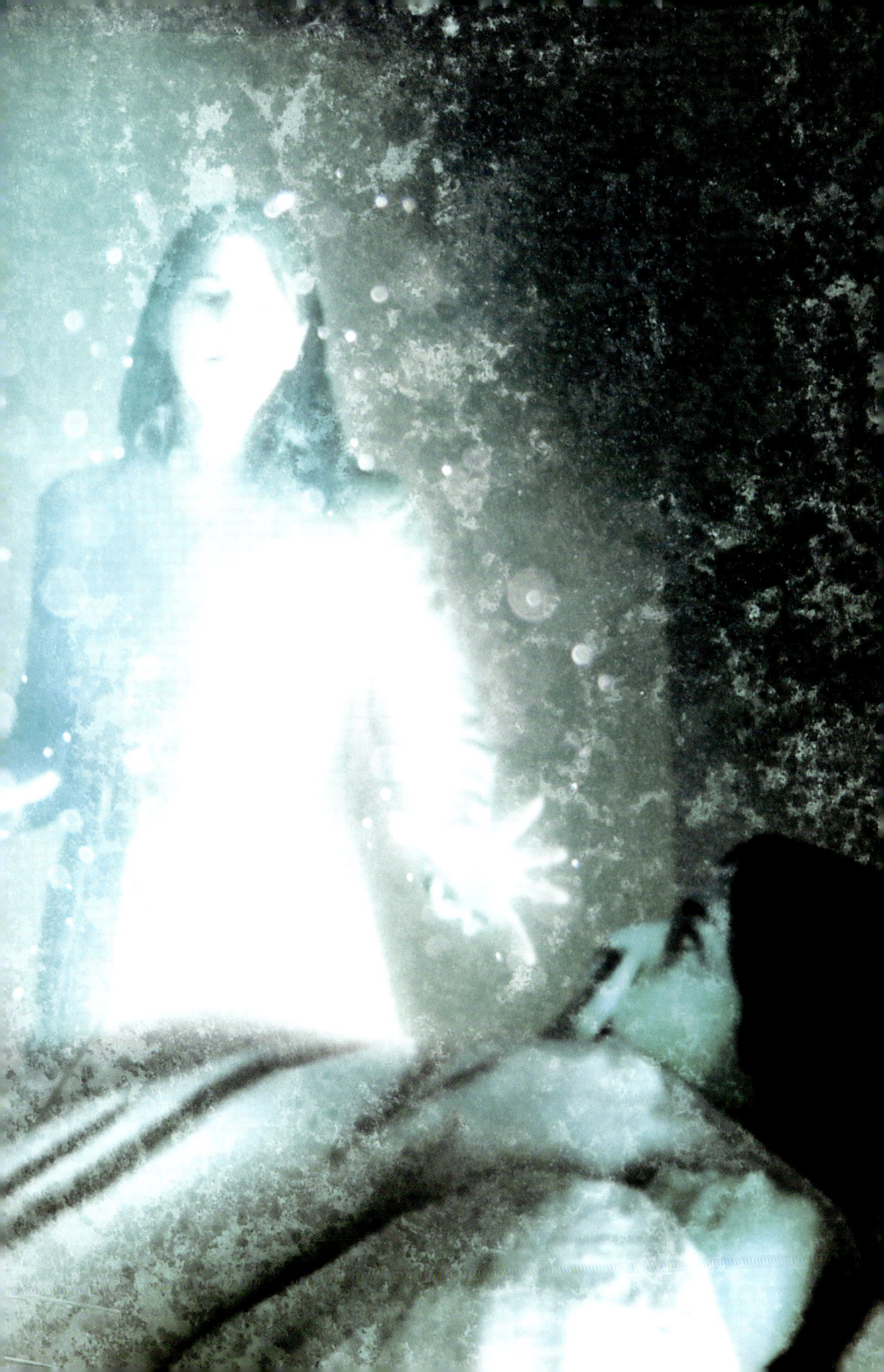

room for him between us and carried on walking.

We were nearly at the main road, when I heard a door slam again, then the sound of feet running towards us. I had known my flatmate for years, and instantly recognised the footsteps as his. Confused, I turned round to see him sprinting to catch up with us. Looking the other way, I saw that the street was completely deserted save for our friend and myself. My first reaction was to wonder how he could have slipped away from us and got to and from our house so quickly. Our friend was equally confused, and it was a while before we understood that my flatmate had only caught up with us the one time.

The weird thing was that we'd both *seen* him out of the corner of our eyes when we'd thought he caught up with us the first time; I'd heard the unmistakable sound of his running feet on both occasions. I knew my flatmate so well that I could spot him in a crowd instantly just from the way he moved, and I'd strongly felt him with me as a real entity. My dinner guest told me that she had also strongly felt his presence. Neither of us could think of a rational explanation.

Lily Mayhew, Plymouth, Devon, 2001

LIE COMES TRUE

A few years back, while working at a software company, I had to go to their California office at fairly short notice. As I didn't at that time have a valid passport and there was little time before I had to go, my boss told me to take the next morning off and go to the passport office in Peterborough to jump the queue and get a passport over the counter rather than wait for a postal application.

That night was my weekly night out with the lads at the pub, and I stayed up later than I should have done. The next morning I overslept considerably, and by the time I'd found my birth certificate and got my photo done it was nearly midday. I was only supposed to take the morning off, and be back at work in the afternoon. I called my boss and told him that I'd just left Peterborough, and that the passport office wouldn't process my application quickly without a letter from my employer saying I needed to travel at short notice. I asked him if he could prepare this so I could come and pick it up and then go back to Peterborough to get the passport. This he did, and I went to my office, collected the letter, and went off to Peterborough, with no one any the wiser.

When I arrived at the passport office and walked into the lobby, the security guard nodded a smile at me and said "Hello again!" Slightly puzzled, but thinking that he'd mistaken me for someone else, I asked what he meant by "again".

> ❝ I'm sure it was you. Looked just like you – same suit, same tie and everything... ❞

He said something like "You were here this morning weren't you?" I said I hadn't been. He then said: "I'm sure it was you. Looked just like you – same suit and tie and everything. Had to go back to work to get a letter from his boss."
Brian Perryman, by email, 2003

CREATURE OF HABIT
About a year and a half ago, a colleague at work had a strange experience that involved me. I used to work for a very small television production company that employed only about 40 staff – so everybody knew everybody else who worked there pretty well. I usually arrived at work around 8am, but on this particular morning I had been asked to come in at 10am. As I walked in, the receptionist cornered me, and asked where I'd been out to. I told her that I'd been at home, but she was adamant that she had already seen me come in at my usual 8am. She had even ticked my name off on her daily register. There was no one else in the company who looked anything like me, and the receptionist couldn't have got me confused with anyone else, as she knew me very well.

   I questioned her on what had happened earlier that morning, and she told me that I had come into reception – wearing exactly the same clothes that I had on as I was questioning her (including a fleece top that I had not worn in her presence before or since) and that I hadn't even said a word to her (which was unusual) but walked straight off towards the studios. She seemed suspicious and thought that I was playing some kind of prank, but I assured her that I was not. After that she appeared quite shocked.
Sharon Mason, by email, 2002

GHOSTS OF PRESAGE

PRE-EMPTIVE SPOTTING
I've had the same odd experience three times in recent months. On each occasion I have seen in the street in central Chichester somebody I thought I recognised as an ex-colleague only to realise, when I was closer, that it was actually not the woman I had thought but a stranger with a slightly similar appearance (height, age, hair colour etc). Then, within minutes, I saw the woman I had at first thought I had seen. In each case the woman was somebody I hadn't seen for a while, and by this I mean years rather than months. In each case there was no way I could have seen the woman in the distance as she was in a different street at the time – indeed, one of them appeared in a car from a side street literally seconds after my mistaken spotting. Also, the women were all acquaintances rather than close friends and had not been in my thoughts at all leading up to the moment. I have no claim to any psychic abilities and wonder if any other readers have experienced similar "pre-emptive" spotting.
Darren Green, Chichester, West Sussex, 2004

MEETING THE FYLGJA
My name is Gunnar, I'm 15 years old and I live in Iceland. Last year, I and my family spent the dark of winter on Nyord, a tiny island in Denmark. A few houses away lived our very good friend Hilmar. One night, I walked over to his house, where my mum was paying a visit. I took the same route as usual, up the street behind the house, through the garden to the backdoor. As I was going through the fence, I saw Hilmar opening the door and scanning the garden. He looked my way, but closed the door, without giving any indication that he had seen me. I came to the door and knocked. He opened it and told me that just a few seconds earlier he and my mum had heard a knock on the door. He looked out but saw nothing.

In the mythology of Iceland such a phenomenon is called a *Fylgja*, a kind of spirit or ghost (or something) accompanying a person and announcing their arrival. It makes its presence known with

noises, the person then comes to mind or pops up in conversation, or the cat announces the person's arrival by certain gestures. Some people have a strong *Fylgja* that clearly precedes their coming. On my way home I met a pitch-black cat under a lampost. It scared me a bit as cats were unheard of on the island. It must have crossed the same crazy bridge as my *Fylgja*.
Gunnar Th Eggertsson, Reykjavik, Iceland, 1997

ADVANCE NOTICE
I was intrigued by Gunnar Eggertsson's letter about the *Fylgja*, the Icelandic ghost of presage. It reminds me of the Norwegian phenomenon of the same kind. They term it *Vardogr* and it is discussed by Brag Steiger in his book *Real Ghosts, Restless Spirits and Haunted Minds*. He writes: "The Vardogr is a kind of spiritual projection which its possessor unconsciously employs to announce his physical arrival." This arrival is, however, announced some minutes before the actual arrival.

As a small boy in a town in south-east Scotland, I lived in a huge, spooky house that had been a Victorian rectory until my parents bought it. My father worked abroad much of the time, my brother had flown the nest and my mother didn't return home from work until 4.30pm or later.

Having got home from school and expecting my mother's arrival at any time, I would regularly hear her car door slam and the front door bang shut. I heard these sounds from afar, so they would be relatively faint, but clearly discernible. I would call hello. Failing to obtain a response, I would come downstairs or come into the hall and investigate. Often enough, I would open the front door and look to see if her car was there.

When I had established that she had not, in fact, arrived, I would then wait for five or 10 minutes, knowing that she was merely letting me know that she was a couple of miles up the road and would shortly be home. I think I experienced this only with her until recently.

On that occasion, my former secretary who worked with me for some years, and who now pops in to collect typing, was due to call by my office. Hearing the buzzer from reception, I went to the door, but she wasn't there. Suspecting a *Vardogr*, I waited for exactly five minutes and then returned to the door. She came around the corner within 30 seconds, startled to see me awaiting her.
Andrew Cray, Edinburgh, 1997

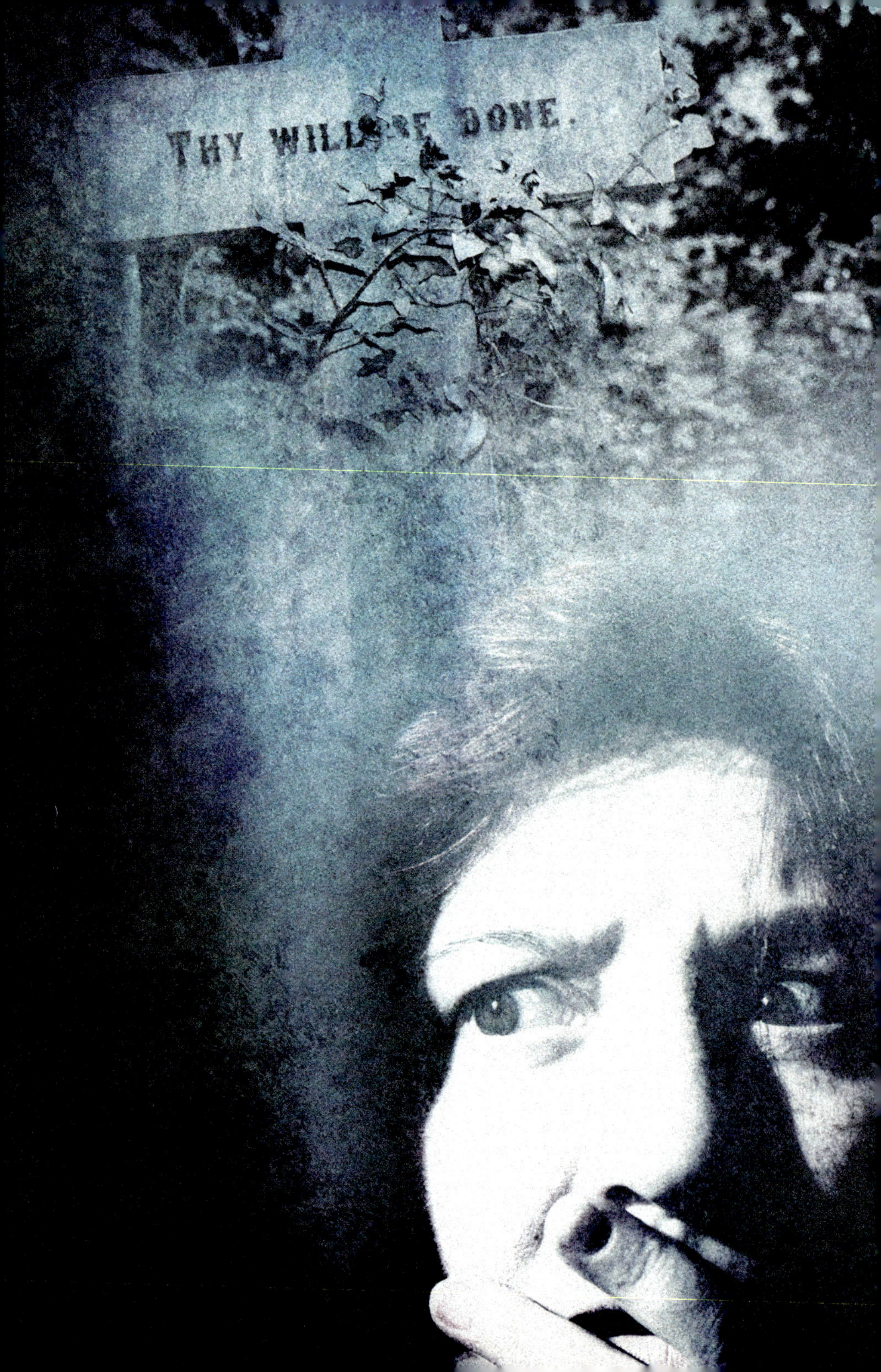
THY WILL BE DONE.

4 *The Sixth Sense*

In moments of crisis, when regular means of communication aren't enough, does the paranormal intervene? Mysterious messages take many forms, from dreams and apparitions to a vision of a grinning skull, the ringing of an alarm clock, Morse Code or the wailing of a banshee: while some are friendly farewells from souls passing over, for the unlucky they can be dark premonitions of death...

PREMONITIONS

THE SIKHS WHO SAW

In 1968, my older brother was 23, and spent most of his time doing up old cars with a friend who lived on a farm. The two young men were working on some old banger when a man in a turban (presumably a Sikh) came to the front of the friend's house. The mother answered the door, and instead of a sales patter, the man looked towards my brother in the corner of the yard and told her: "I feel very sorry for that boy's parents, they are going to have sorrow in the family soon." About one week later my brother crashed on his way home, breaking his neck. He was in a coma for nearly one week before he died.

A year or so later, another Sikh came calling, this time at our front door. He looked at my mother, and indicated with his hands the graduated size of her family (there were six of us); when he came to the second eldest – my dead brother – he stopped, and looked concerned. He then pointed to my mother's eye, and seemed to indicate some sort of problem. Not long after, she developed glaucoma in that eye.

There are other incidents connected with the death of my brother, like the appearance of a hospital odour in our house, noted by both my parents and heavily redolent of the week they spent at his bedside. My mother once heard a car draw up outside the house, and my brother call out for her. When she went outside, there was no car in the road.

My parents, although both practising Catholics, had recourse to the spirit-in-the-glass, and seemed to get some results: the glass indicated that the cause of the accident had been a pile of discarded road-builder's tarmac on the roadside, a fact confirmed later by another of my brothers. A set of my dead brother's house keys were found by similar means, as the glass directed them behind the gas fire (where the keys had evidently fallen). It also appeared that my brother's sense of humour survived his departure from this mortal coil. His widow made a lemon meringue pie, a pastry confection that he loathed in life. She left it to cool, and returned to find that the pie had been turned upside down and squashed on the table.
Philip Hoare, London, 1996

PURPLE PREMONITION

At the age of 14, in 1978, I was trying to settle into a new school and was getting bullied by Karen and her gang. She drove me to tears and distraction by tripping me up, stealing my sandwiches and spitting in my drink. She was a rough girl who swore and I was scared stiff of her.

One day she tripped me down a flight of stairs and started laughing. I looked up and found that her face had turned into a grinning skull. Instead of crying I stared in astonishment, which replaced her laughter with a puzzled expression.

Afterwards, I dreamed that she was standing on a bridge. I did my best to avoid her, but I couldn't and was instead drawn like a magnet to where she stood. It occurred to me that I couldn't cross the bridge anyway because there was a line dividing it, and I knew I couldn't step over. She smiled at me, then turned away and vanished. I remember her hair was a strange purple colour, a colour that is still vivid and fresh in my mind.

Two weeks later, she was killed instantly when a car hit her on the way home from a party. Before she'd gone out that night she had dyed her short cropped hair bright purple.
Linda Hardy, Wellingborough, Northamptonshire, 1998

DREAMING OF RABBITS

I have often had vivid dreams, which a couple of days later have turned out to be true, but have largely dismissed them, and put them down to chance. However, I

THE SIXTH SENSE IT HAPPENED TO ME!

> " *I looked up and found that Karen's face had turned into a grinning skull* "

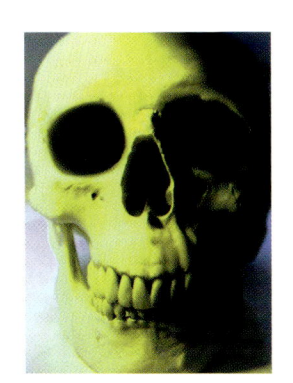

had a particularly vivid dream recently. In it, a really strong gust of wind blew the top off a rabbit hutch, and I was running around the garden trying to catch the rabbits. I came down to breakfast in the morning, and started telling my family about the dream. As I did so, I opened up the morning paper and turned to a story about a freak hurricane that had hit a very small area in Britain. It focused on a human-interest story of a family who had found the top blown off their rabbit hutch, and had had to chase the rabbits around the garden. Even my family had to admit it was a strange coincidence!

There is said to be a history of sixth sense in my family. My great grandfather was the seventh son of a seventh son, and had the gift of second sight. His gift was so impressive that he was employed to help police investigations. He would often have premonitions, and would send warnings to members of the family. He wrote to my other great grandmother and warned her that she must keep her son (my grandfather) away from water at all costs. He had had a vision where her son was being pulled out of the water with a stick. Being very superstitious, she followed this advice to the letter, and my grandfather was not allowed near water. However, one day whilst holidaying by the sea, my grandfather disappeared. A huge storm brewed and they were very worried and went out searching for him. Hours later, my bedraggled grandfather appeared with an old man. The latter had been walking by the pier when he saw a huge wave engulf it, carrying my grandfather off into the sea. Running to save him, the man had eventually managed to drag him back by stretching out his walking stick, and getting him to hold onto it.

Anna Smith, Bristol, 2005

PARTING SHOTS

LAST ORDERS
Shortly after Easter one year, my wife and I went to Blackpool for a long weekend. After dinner on Friday, my wife retired to our rented apartment and I went to the Old Bridge Inn at the top of the road and ordered a pint of Boddingtons. I saw a man at the end of the bar watching me. Eventually he walked over. "Excuse me for staring," he said, "but do you come from South Yorkshire?"

"I was born there," I replied, "but we moved to North Yorkshire 20 years ago, although my sister and brothers still live near Barnsley."

"Your name isn't Norman by any chance?" he asked.

I was stunned: "Yes it is actually."

"Well I'm Jimmy Marriot," he replied.

Suddenly the penny dropped. When we were kids Jimmy lived next door but two to us in Goldthorpe, a small pit village near Barnsley. Jimmy, being the oldest by three years, was the leader of our gang.

I ordered two more pints and we talked about the old days. He asked about my sister, who he used to fancy. Eventually the landlord rang the bell and we arranged to meet the following evening as he wanted me to introduce him to my wife. With that we said goodnight.

I told my wife the strange story next morning and we decided to go to the pub at about 8.30 that evening. There was no sign of Jimmy. I asked the landlord if he had seen the bloke I had been talking to the previous night.

"Sorry," he replied, "I saw you come in but I didn't see you talking to anyone." We waited until 9.30pm, drank up and went for a walk around town thinking no more of it.

When we were back home on the Monday, my sister rang, which she has done like clockwork for years, with the news and gossip, as we don't get down to see her very much. She asked how the weekend went and I told her about meeting her old friend Jimmy Marriot. She was silent for a moment, then she said, "Are you trying to be funny? Because if you are it's in very bad taste." Very quietly she told me that Jimmy Marriot had been killed in a car accident on his way home from work just outside Barnsley at 6.30 on Friday night.

Norman Green, Robin Hood Bay, North Yorkshire, 1996

BIRDS OF A FEATHER

A terminally ill person made a special arrangement for her parrot to stay at the vet's where my daughter works, so that she could visit it regularly. The bird settled well and became a great friend of all the girls working there. It remained there for over a year, perfectly well and happy, until one day it became sick and, as my daughter carried it to the vet, it died. The whole practice was shocked and upset. Tears were shed but, when they attempted to contact the owner (yes, you've guessed it), they discovered that she had suffered a relapse and had died the same afternoon as her beloved pet.

Pam Thornton, Llandegla, Denbighshire, 1998

DREAM FAREWELL

During the long and pleasant summer of 1960, when I was seven years old, I passed the house of an old lady each morning on my way to school. She was usually in a rickety old chair on her front porch. "Good morning, Mrs Thorpe," I would call and she would say: "Good morning, Peter."

One night near the end of the school year, I dreamed I was walking to school past Mrs Thorpe's house. She was there as usual, sitting on her porch, and I noticed with detachment that she had no face. Despite this I called out as usual: "Good morning, Mrs Thorpe" and in return I heard a voice that was calm and kindly but devastating nonetheless: "Goodbye Peter". I sat upright in bed, breathless and sweating. After a moment I lay down again and was soon asleep.

The next morning, as I packed my satchel for school, my mother told me in a hushed voice that Mrs Thorpe had been taken ill during the night and had died. Even though I was young boy I knew I had been privileged. Mrs Thorpe had come to me in death and bid me farewell. I never told anyone of my experience that night until I was a grown man.

Peter Lloyd, Salisbury, Wiltshire, 1999

CRY OF THE BANSHEE?

In 1999, around midnight, unable to sleep, I went down to the kitchen to make a drink. As soon as I got there, a loud haunting, wailing sound began. Despite being painfully loud, it couldn't be heard in any other part of the house, even in the next room, which had no door between it and the kitchen. It couldn't have been caused by wind, as it was a very still night. No equipment, electrical or other, had been left on. After several minutes, the sound rose to an almost unbearable scream before quickly dying down to nothing.

The next day we discovered my great aunt had died in her bed, sometime between 11pm and 1am the previous night. Had I heard the cry of the banshee lamenting the approaching death of my relative?
Simon Day, Longhill, Humberside, 2005

INTERCEPT MESSAGE

In about 1960 I was based at an RAF training school at Wythall, near Lincoln, training to become an intercept operator. The job was to monitor potential enemy communications; training included taking Morse code at relatively high speeds through interference and the use of more than one receiver at the same time. It culminated in attempting to intercept, using two receivers, a number of very short messages sent via a local loop by the instructors. The frequencies were unknown to the trainees, who had to twiddle the dials and write down what they could.

If I remember correctly after nearly 50 years, I managed to intercept 10 messages. I came out top, but the instructors said that one of the messages I had written down – "Come immediately VIP" – hadn't been sent by them. Since by then I realised that I had passed, I made no comment on this mysterious message.

A year earlier, I had returned from Australia, where I had served six years in the Australian Army, as my mother was seriously ill with cancer. She had improved somewhat after my return so I felt no problem in returning to service life, albeit in a different service. After passing the intercept course, I returned home, and was horrified to be told that my mother had died of the cancer at the very time I had received the "come immediately" message. My sister said she hadn't attempted to phone me, as she knew that I was due home that day anyway.

Did I get an electronic message from the beyond, or was it the result of a subconscious anxiety on my part? Now at age 81 I often wonder if I was informed of the death by radiotelegraphy.
Robert Moyes, Gislingham, Suffolk, 2007

> *My mother had died of cancer at the very time I had received the message...*

HELPING HANDS

In 1951, when I was three years old, three adult-sized figures glided, rather than walked, down the hallway and through the closed and locked front door during the night when it was dark. All three glowed softly. The centre one seemed weak, being helped and supported by the person on either side. How was I able to see them clearly while my body was asleep upstairs in a cot? Why did they all ignore me, standing only a few feet away? How did they get through the door?

Next morning my mother explained that my uncle, in whose home we were staying, had died in his sleep. Years later I learned that he had had a massive heart attack. I tried to explain to the shocked and grieving adults who gathered for the funeral that I had seen uncle with two 'helpers', but my vocabulary was sorely deficient. Who would listen to a child? Most of those unheeding folk have since died.

Were the figures I saw 'angels' coming to fetch my uncle's soul? If it was just a dream, why have I remembered it so vividly for almost 50 years?
Valerie A Riddell, Turriff, Aberdeenshire, 1999

CRISIS APPARITIONS

In 2002, my mother was unfortunate enough to contract Legionnaire's Disease and spent several weeks in hospital. For the majority of this time she was sedated with morphine and completely unconscious. Her illness was so bad that her family and friends were prepared for the worst.

As the disease took an increasingly powerful hold, people around my mother started to experience strange things. Her next-door neighbour, a good friend, was in her back garden one day bending down to pull weeds out of the ground

IT HAPPENED TO ME! THE SIXTH SENSE

when she became aware of a presence next to her and looked up to see my mother standing nearby watching her work. The image vanished, but not before the neighbour had time to get a good look at my mother and even recognise the clothes that she was wearing, (not the nightie that she was actually wearing in hospital but some of her ordinary clothes).

A few days after this, my aunt was also visited by my mother in her house and once again was able to get a very clear view of her before the image disappeared. As before, my mother was just standing beside her appearing to take an interest in what my aunt was doing.

I never saw this ghostly image of my mother, but she did manifest for me in other ways. After visiting her in hospital, I would come home to find the TV switched on (I had definitely switched it off before leaving the house) and it would be busily changing channels by itself. It would also have the annoying habit of switching channels in the middle of the programme I was watching.

A few days after the visions mentioned above, my boyfriend was relaxing in the bath one evening when suddenly he had an overwhelming urge to get out and stand in the middle of the bathroom. He did this and was rewarded with the sound of a loud groan which he was sure came from my mother. He told me that it felt as though she wanted to tell him that things had changed and she was going to be OK.

We later found out that it was about this time that my mother suddenly stopped getting worse. Within a few days she even began to get better and has now thankfully made a full recovery.

She has no memory of her various apparitions, but says that the morphine produced many hallucinations and bizarre dreams. As soon as she regained full consciousness the problems with my TV stopped and have not recurred. It seems strange that someone can appear as a ghost whilst still living, but I feel that the severity of my mother's illness and the huge amount of morphine that she was given (the hospital gave her extra amounts in the expectation that she was not going to pull through) combined to allow her to leave her body in spirit form and visit those closest to her.

This has, however, left my boyfriend with the worrying impression that when my mother does finally shuffle off the mortal coil, neither of us will get a moment's peace.
Alison Derrick, Herefordshire, 2003

CLOCK COMMUNICATIONS

MARKING TIME
Back in 1985, a business I was running was in a very bad way financially. I managed to conceal my problems from my parents, being determined to battle through on my own and not cause them concern.

My mother called me one Sunday morning, offering me some cash totally out of the blue. I declined the offer, but she said "I want to give it to you before I die," which was a very strange statement to come from my perfectly healthy mother. I went to my parents' home that afternoon to find my mother reminiscing over the "old days", which was another strange shift in her outlook. I left the house at 2.30pm and precisely an hour later, my mother rose from her chair, collapsed and died from a heart attack. At the inquest, it was declared that she had been perfectly fit, with no evidence of any previous heart trouble.

After the funeral 10 days later, I went back to my parents' house for the wake. On the mantelpiece sat a carriage clock driven by four revolving bearings. I remember that as a young lad of four I had been mesmerised by the to-and-fro action of the clock's mechanism. It had never broken down or stopped in the 40 years that it had been on the mantelpiece – until the day of the funeral. It stopped at 3.30pm, the time of the funeral and the exact time my mother had died.

It remained stuck at 3.30 for five years until one afternoon, sitting with my father, I noticed that it was now showing 10.30. I mentioned this to my father who said that he'd cleaned it that morning and must have freed the jammed mechanism. However, it moved no more. The next morning, my father went shopping, fell down and died from a heart attack at 10.30am. The clock now sits in my house and has never moved since that time.
CN Satterthwaite, Sollhull, West Midlands, 1997

TOLD BY THE CLOCK
My son died in Guy's Hospital, London, on 5 April 2004. The time on his death certificate is 5.04am. On that morning, my alarm clock went off at 5.02 or 5.03. It has never rung at the wrong time before or since, over several years. The tone was slightly lower than usual. It woke me and I got out of bed to turn it off. It is far enough away to make sure I do not ignore it or go back to sleep. It would not turn

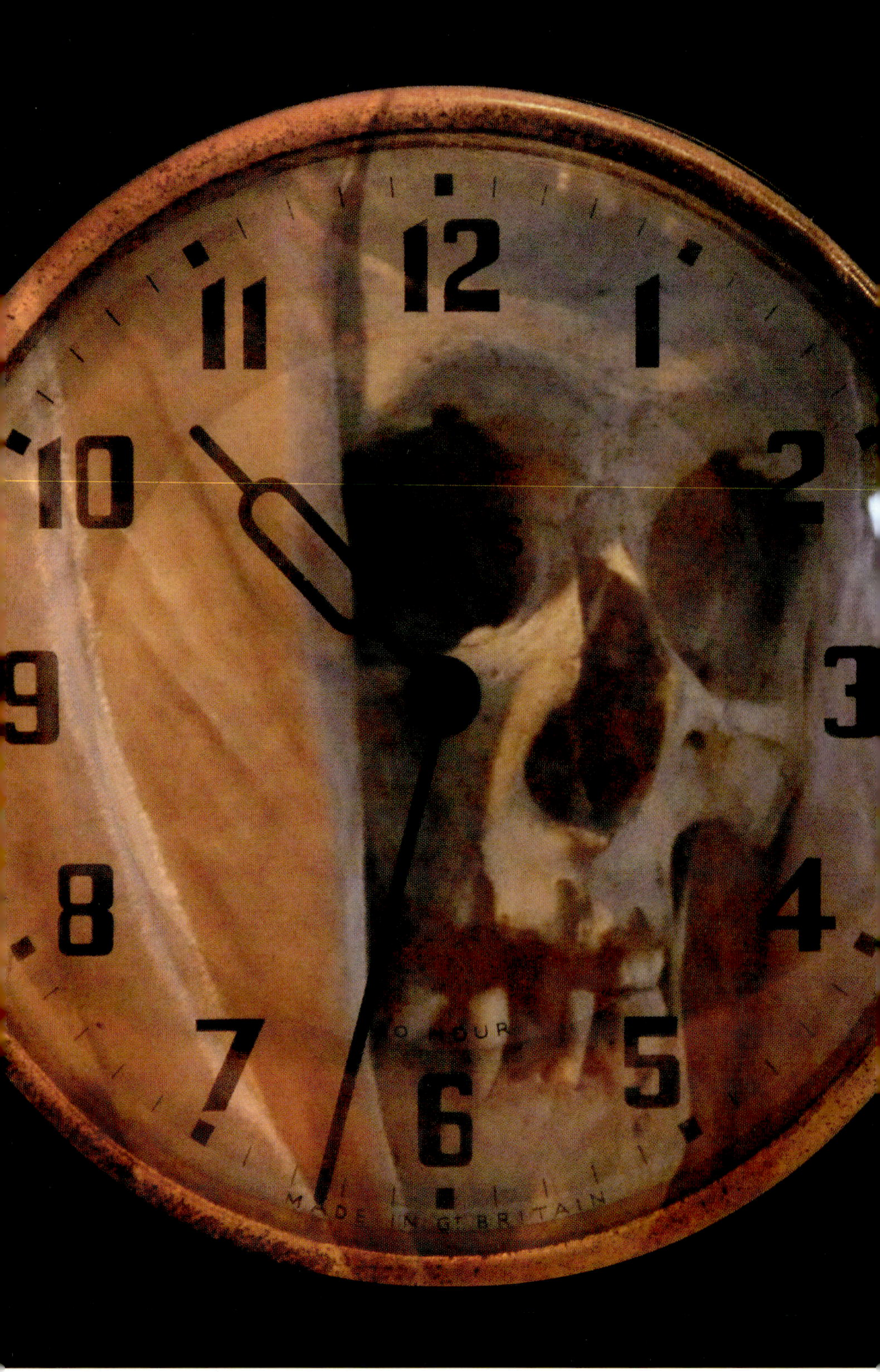
MADE IN Gt BRITAIN

off but made this different sound for a few minutes while I shook it and turned it on and off, trying to prevent it from waking my husband so early.

I looked at the alarm setting, which said 5.45, the time for which it is always set. Then the ringing stopped. I checked that it would still wake me at 5.45 and went back to sleep. At 5.15 the same thing happened again. It rang, I got up to stop it but could not, just as before. After another few minutes sleep I woke with the correct sound at the correct time. At 6.30 my daughter rang me with the dreadful news.

It was then I realised that the unusual alarm bell was my son contacting me to say his body and spirit had separated and his soul, mind, personality, consciousness or intellect – whatever you call this part of a human being – was still alive, able to remain on Earth for 10 minutes or so in preparation for the journey to Heaven. The second call was probably when this process was completed and he left the Earth, living, still able to find and recognise his mother, travelling through time and space instantly. My son chose the clock because he used to mend clocks until they became so disposable that it was not worth the bother, unless they were antiques. He knew I would associate the clock with him.

Eileen Denham, Chatham, Kent, 2004

WATCH SEEKS OWNER

My grandfather drowned in a canal – whether suicide or accident was never established. When the body surfaced after about two weeks, his pocket watch was obviously beyond economic repair. However, a family friend who happened to be a watchmaker agreed to undertake the work, provided no time limit was placed upon it.

After about six months, the watch was returned and given to me, but it refused to work for more than a few hours. The watchmaker checked it, found no fault, and my father took it on with the same result. He gave up on it and hung it on a hook in his workshop.

Some months later, my cousin, who was partially sighted, came on a visit. During holidays from the School for the Blind he had visited my grandfather and gone on walks with him. He recognised the watch and said it had been promised to him. My father said, "Then you must have it", but warned him that it didn't work.

You can guess the result – the watch kept perfect time for my cousin for many years until his death.

SA Skinner, Watford, Hertfordshire, 1999

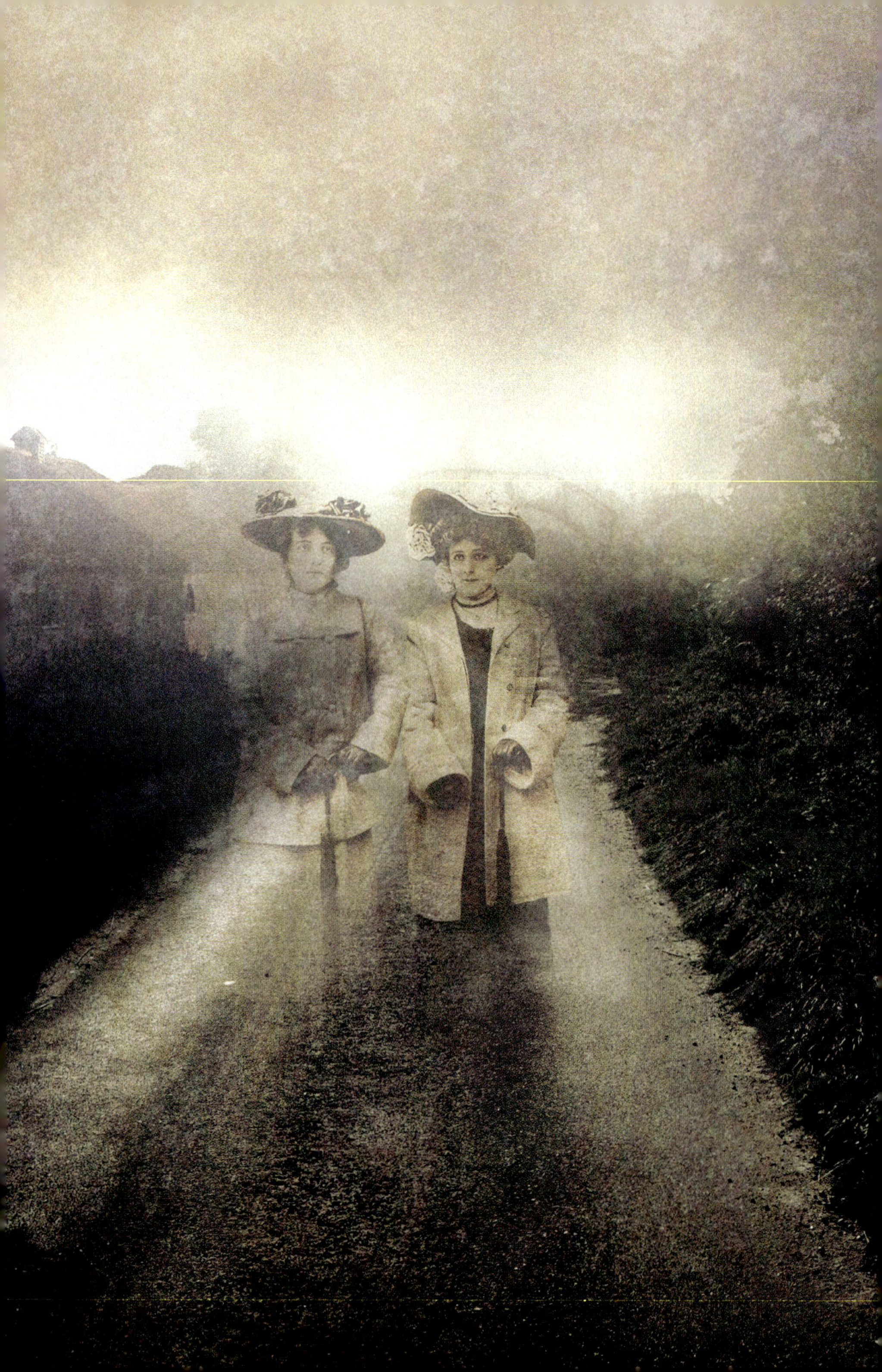

5 Timeslips

Common sense tells us that time moves inexorably in one direction and we are confined to the present. The past, we believe, is out of our reach; but on rare occasions some of us appear to glimpse scenes from yesteryear. And time can play other tricks: the same sequence of events can repeat like a tape loop, or everything around us appears to slow right down or even come to a halt.

HISTORICAL VISIONS

ROMAN CAVALRY RETURNS

For almost five years, John England and I have gone metal detecting on 2,000 acres of land belonging to a country estate near the village of Little Wenlock outside Telford in Shropshire. One warm Autumn evening in the first week of October 1995, we made the half-hour drive and, after cooking up two tins of beans, decided to search a large field which had never produced much, but we felt it had potential; just a gut feeling. We called it the boulder field, because of a pile of boulders in one corner.

Shortly before midnight, we began to sweep our search heads over the ancient landscape. John headed off on his usual perimeter route while I made a diagonal across the field. The silence was broken by the occasional 'clunk' as my search-head hit a stone. The first half dozen signals produced nothing but iron, but then I unearthed a silver coin. The profile of an elephant told me it was a republican denarius of Julius Caesar. Over the next hour I found several Roman bronzes and another denarius, this time of Rutilius Flaccus.

Three hours after we began the search, I met John, who had found seven coins and a fibula. We flopped down on a grassy bank for tea and sandwiches. Getting our second wind, we resumed the search together and discovered four artefacts

65

within 40 minutes. One had "Nigel" punched on its surface and was obviously a javelin tip. Suddenly, we heard a noise like galloping horses. The ground vibrated as the thundering hooves came right at us. The noise passed between us as we ran in opposite directions and died away as quickly as it had started. We had not seen anything.

A little unnerved, we headed across the field towards the car. Half way across, we came upon what looked like a hedge, although we knew there was no such obstruction in the boulder field. It was about 9ft (2.7m) tall, very dense, with a straight top as if it had been cut; brown in colour, with traces of white on top.

Thinking we must have strayed in the dark, we walked next to it for almost 80 yards. By the time we had come to the end, we were able to look down the slope of the field and see the car. Realising that we were indeed in the boulder field, we turned round to find that the 'hedge' had disappeared.

We waited for dawn by the car and then spent the best part of an hour examining the field. The winter wheat had yet to break the surface; our own footprints showed up, but nothing else. These clearly showed how we had been forced to deviate from our route. From a diagonal course, we had gone off at a tangent for almost 100 yards before resuming our original direction.

A few weeks later, we called on archæologist Mike Stokes at Rowley House Museum, Shrewsbury. He was very interested in our finds and their location. There was no record of any Roman sites in that area. The javelin tip was one of the best he had seen and the only one inscribed in such a personal way. "Nigel" was presumably short for "Nigelus". The other artefacts were bridle fittings used by Roman cavalry.

I believe that John and I witnessed a time slip and that the 'hedge' was really a stockade surrounding a fort. Could the sound of hooves have come from a cavalry unit coming from (or returning to) the fort?

Colin Ayling, Woodside, Shropshire, 1996

> **" The scene changed: the cemetery was neat, the railings newly painted "**

MANCHESTER REWIND

In early 1983, when I was 49, I travelled to the Cheetham area of Manchester for my son's wedding. The day before the ceremony, I walked to the church to become familiar with the route. I had never been to Manchester before. Glancing across a main road, I saw a rather dilapidated cemetery with rusty railings, very long grass and what I took to be a chapel with a square tower. I can't recall if I glanced away and then returned my gaze, or if what took place happened before my eyes. Suddenly the scene changed: the cemetery was neat; the streaked and dirty yellow brickwork clean; the railings newly painted. The clouds were replaced by blue sky and sunshine.

Several figures were walking quite quickly along an unseen path to my right. There were two women about 30 years old; the one nearer to me had her hair up, with a small, circular hat of flowers and a cream-coloured parasol to shade her and her companion. She wore a long tight white dress that swung from side to side in a corkscrewing motion, a frilly blouse with a high collar and white gloves almost to her elbows. Her companion was shorter, with loose, shoulder-length hair. They were in animated conversation, too far away for me to overhear. Other figures on the path, about 20ft (6m) before and behind this couple, were less clear. Very quickly the whole scene vanished and the drab present-day returned.

About 10 or 15 minutes later I reached a road junction. Opposite was a patio area bordered by four or five modern-fronted shops set in a semi-circle. I scanned other shops to my right and turned once more to the patio, ready to cross the busy road when traffic allowed. It now had four or five wooden tables set with chairs. Several men were sitting at the tables, dressed poorly in thick grey flannel and large flat caps. The shops behind them looked empty with sparse window displays, I'm not certain of what.

Around the edge of the pavement were three raised steps, with bollards at about 6ft (1.8m) intervals. The whole scene was grey, rather like an old photograph. I had the impression that the men were outside a public house or a café. They were in conversation, but I could hear nothing, not even the modern traffic passing me. A sense of "unworldliness" pervaded and yet it seemed familiar in some way. Then it all vanished, to be replaced by the modern scene.

Derek Gibson, Wadebridge, Cornwall, 1999

EPIC FOREST

Some years ago, I used to drive regularly from Ilford [Essex] to Hornsey [north London] to visit my sister-in-law, always taking the same route. On one rainy afternoon in about 1983, I was driving with my husband and we approached a certain junction on the Woodford New Road. I had to be in the outside lane ready to approach traffic lights in the wide road, prior to turning right – the only turning at this T junction. The approach to these lights involved a bend in the road and on turning the bend, we were confronted with a totally unfamiliar scene.

Instead of traffic lights there was a small grass triangle with a wooden signpost that we didn't have time to read. Having no alternative, we turned right and found ourselves lost. The weather was dark and rainy and there was a bank of trees on either side of the road. We came to a fork in the lane, and there was another wooden signpost pointing to Walthamstow and a few yards ahead we could see a normal road and people, so we drove towards it. We were out of our way but finally were directed back to our intended course.

I firmly believe we were in a time warp of some kind. The whole thing lasted, I suppose, about three or four minutes. I would love to know what this 'lost' area was like years ago before it was altered and traffic lights introduced. It is easy enough to take a wrong turn, but there is no other turn to take at this junction and those who know the area can't explain what we might have done.

Mrs JM Green, Ilford, Essex, 1992

TIME-LAPSE ENCOUNTER

In the summer of 1988 or 1989 when I was 18 or 19, I used to go out with a girl who lived about two miles away in the Greater Manchester area. There were two ways to get there, one through a semi-rural area, the other along a main road. As it was a pleasant summer's evening, I decided to take the semi-rural route. Around seven o'clock, I passed a farmhouse and was approaching a bridge over a railway when walking towards me I noticed a man wearing plus-fours, a flat cap and pushing an old-fashioned wooden wheelbarrow. As he came nearer, we started to look at each other with a sense of puzzlement. As I had long hair, I was used to being looked at in a strange manner and for my part, he did look rather odd. Assuming he was from the farm, I carried on walking.

Then two women dressed in what I can only describe as late Victorian/early Edwardian dresses and wide brimmed hats came walking towards me. Again, we regarded one another with a sense of bemusement without uttering a word and passed each other by.

After taking a few more steps, I turned around for another look, assuming by this stage I had happened upon some guests on their way to a fancy-dress party. They had disappeared. There wasn't time for them to have reached the farmhouse, which was the nearest building. Unless they had darted into a field and hid behind a wall, there was no way they could have disappeared from view so quickly.

Feeling a bit shaken, I hurried on to my girlfriend's where my tale was greeted with a certain degree of mockery. The area where I lived was not up for historical re-enactments and this style of clothing was certainly not *de rigeur* in late 1980s Greater Manchester.
Lee Stansfield, Stockport, 2003

INDIAN ON THE HIGHWAY
In the summer of 1985, I was working for the Kansas Department of Transportation doing traffic studies at the intersections of remote rural highways. It was a dull job, but it afforded me some time to read and earn some money for college.

One particular hot July afternoon, I found myself doing a traffic study overlooking the Smokey Hill river valley in west central

Kansas. It had been a rather uneventful day. All of a sudden I heard a very high-pitched noise akin to electronic feedback. My first reaction was to turn down the car radio, which I did to no avail. The irritating sound seemed to come from the back of the vehicle, so I got out to investigate. As I walked down the road, a movement to my right caught my eye. I turned my head and saw an Indian on a horse coming down the highway embankment. This was not a modern-day Native American, but an Indian brave circa 1840. He was naked except for a leather loincloth and a pair of moccasins and was riding bareback without any conventional bridle, just a rope tied around the pony's head. In his right hand was an antique-looking rifle and in his left the rope.

The sight took my breath away and all I could think of was saying "Hi!" He ignored me as if I were not there. As he approached the far side of the road, he stopped and intently scanned the river valley below. I turned to see what he was looking at. Down in the valley was a large herd of buffalo [bison] strung out for miles. This sight made my head swim because the mighty herds of buffalo had been exterminated in Kansas over a century ago.

I caught my breath and turned back to observe the Indian, but he was gone. I ran over to where I had last seen him and looked down the hill. There was no sign of the Indian and now no trace of the buffalo either. As the hot sun beat down on me, I slowly walked back to the car and noticed that the annoying sound was absent, too.

Keith Manies, by email, 2002

RERUNS AND SLOWDOWNS

PENSIONERS SEE DOUBLE

The following happened to Jack and I, both senior citizens now, sober and sane! We go for our walk along Finchley Road, eastwards towards Swiss Cottage [in north London], circa 4-5pm, most days. We walk slowly and observantly, neither of us wear glasses and we both have keen vision. Several times, we have seen things double...

A few months ago, walking past the Post Office, going east, we saw a most unusual male – tall, wearing some kind of bright red anorak, with a springy walk. No one took any notice of him. Then a few yards further along the road, we saw this

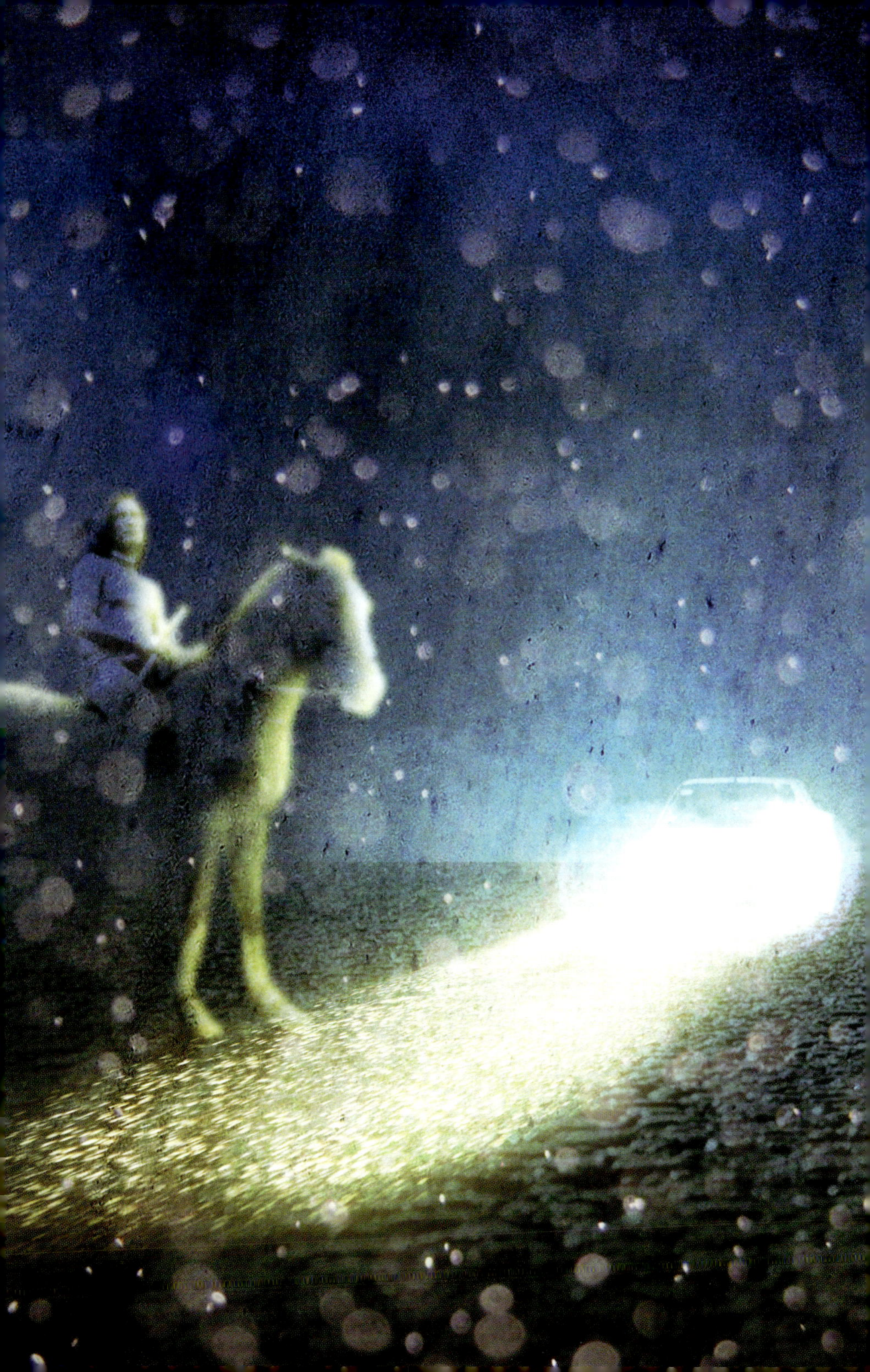

very same man coming out of Boots the chemist. He could not have run back in the time. A few weeks ago, a blind woman walked by us, (with white stick) and I drew aside slightly so as not to brush against her. Then walking on eastward, a few minutes later we saw her crossing the road at a lights crossing. Again she couldn't have dodged past, as like the man in red she was coming towards us. Another time, we saw Idries Shah and girlfriend (whom we know) in this street, getting into their car, he smoking a cigar. We walked on and then a few minutes later, saw Idries Shah and the girl walking towards us... no cigar and no car... The last occurrence was bizarre. Walking eastwards again, we saw a woman in black, wheeling an idiot woman in white in a wheelchair... woman was lolling on one side, looking vacant. Then walking eastwards, we saw again, coming towards us, this very same couple! This time I noticed a small cross on the woman in black. This so shocked Jack he murmured, "I wonder how they managed that one!"

We have had some other incidents like this but years ago; this latest batch have all been within a few months. It certainly adds a spice to our walks! Are we seeing into the immediate past? Which is the real sighting – first time or second time?

Judith Gee, Hampstead, London, 1980

MAN IN BROWN

At about 8:30am one morning recently, I was travelling towards my office on Chaffron Way in Milton Keynes. It was a bright sunny day and the roads were busy with the usual volume of traffic. Approaching Saxon Street at the Eaglestone Roundabout I slowed to give way to the cars on my right and to my left I caught sight of a pedestrian – fairly unusual along the dual carriageways in Milton Keynes unless you are near the local college or various schools. He was about 5ft 4in (1.60m), possibly Asian but certainly dark-haired with a side parting, wearing a brown suit, oversized brown glasses and carrying a brown briefcase – my overall impression was that he had stepped straight out of the 1970s. In the few seconds that I watched him he marched purposefully along the grass verge, but his whole trajectory seemed wrong as his path would have taken him directly across the roundabout. The traffic cleared, I carried on to work and thought little further of it.

However, returning home that evening at about 5:45pm, I was approaching the Eaglestone Roundabout along Chaffron Way from the opposite direction

> **" My overall impression was that he had stepped straight out of the 1970s "**

when I caught sight of the same man, wearing the same clothes, in the same place that I had seen him that morning and marching along on exactly the same route. It was like watching the same clip of film but from a different perspective.

I got home and puzzled over it for a while. Eventually, I told my husband who helpfully suggested that the man might just have been walking in circles whilst my father suggested that I had had my first encounter with the "men in brown". I've kept an eye out every morning and evening for the past month or so, but have not seen him again. Indeed, I've never seen anyone else at that particular junction.

Tania Morgan, Middleton, Buckinghamshire, 2004

TIME-TRAVELLING FATTY

About two years ago I was driving down County Road in Kirkdale, Liverpool, towards the city. The traffic was fairly heavy as people were returning home in the early evening. I pulled up at the Spellow Lane traffic lights, which were on red – I was about four cars back from the lights in the outside lane. I then noticed a rather large, plump woman in a garish outfit cutting through the stationary cars to cross the road. She walked immediately in front of my car, from left to right, before crossing when there was a gap in the oncoming traffic. With her blonde hair worn up on her head and her attire, this middle-aged woman was very remarkable in appearance, arguably for the wrong reasons. The lights changed and I set off down Walton Road into Kirkdale Road, with the traffic flowing quickly. I then had to stop at the traffic lights with Great Homer Street – which are about three-quarters of a mile (1.2km) from Spellow Lane.

To my amazement the same woman cut through the stationary vehicles, immediately in front of my car, from left to right. There was no mistaking her, unless she had a twin sister who dressed identically. There is no way I can conceive for the woman to have got from the first position to the second in what must have been about 90 seconds, given the absence of transport. I am baffled.
Rob Gandy, Bebington, Wirral, 1992

LOST ON GROUNDHOG DAY
About five years ago, my ex-girlfriend was working in a bar in the centre of Dublin. She usually worked until the bar closed and would then walk about a mile home to the flat she was sharing on the outskirts of the city. One night as she was walking home, a car pulled up slowly behind her, the driver pulled down the window and asked her for the directions to a nearby hotel. She gave the man directions, walked home and went to bed, thinking nothing of this brief incident. However, the following night, at *exactly* the same time, in *exactly* the same place, the *same* man, wearing the *same* clothes asked her for the *same* directions and headed off that way once again. Needless to say, it freaked the hell out of her as it did to me.
Jamie Davis, Dalkey, Co. Dublin, 2003

JUMP LEAD MYSTERY
Last summer my partner and I were driving west on the M4. Somewhere near Reading, traffic ground to a halt due to an accident. For the best part of an hour we moved in stops and starts, rarely making more than 20 yards each time. During one of the stops, we were next to two very expensive low-slung black sports cars parked one in front of the other on the hard shoulder. The cars were in show-room condition, sleek and immaculate. Each had its bonnet open and the cars were connected by bright yellow jump-leads. The two drivers were standing on the grass verge chatting.

We continued our slow crawl west. After a while, conditions improved and the traffic was moving at around 40-60 mph (64-96km/h). Somewhere around Junction 12 we passed the identical cars, parked on the hard shoulder with their bonnets open and connected by the same bright yellow jump-leads. Even assuming that one of them had a severe battery problem which needed constant re-charging, the only way they could have passed us would have been by driving at full speed down the hard shoulder. This, I think, we would have noticed.
Mike Harding, by email, 2002

STILL LIFE

On Saturday, 9 June 2007, my wife and I were first out of St Joseph's parish church in Worksop (Nottinghamshire) because we were in a terrific rush. Mass started at 6pm and finished at 7pm, but my wife, a nurse, starts work at 8pm. In the intervening hour we have to cook and eat, take the dogs for a walk, get changed and (in her case) drive to work.

It was hot and oppressive. In our haste we failed to acknowledge various friends (who on reflection were staring at us dumbly), but no problem, we would see them the following week. It struck me that everyone was a bit, well, slow... or was it me who was in such a rush? We got into the car, I fired up, and turned into Wessex Road to do a U-turn in the mouth of the road. Halfway through my 'U', some fellow turned up and stopped at the junction. I waited for him to move on. And waited... And waited. Why didn't he move? No one was coming, the road was clear. I looked at him. He was frozen with his mouth open. Everyone else was frozen too!

A man with a black Labrador stood ramrod straight; his dog, also frozen, had a stick clamped in its jaws. Everyone and everything was motionless – except my wife and me. I just whipped round everything and drove away. "What's up with people?" my wife remarked. "They'd move fast enough if they had to be at work in half an hour." I looked in my mirror and everyone was moving again.

It was uncomfortably hot – and quiet. I don't even recall birds singing – nothing – it all seemed kind of muffled, distant. I'm not claiming that time stood still – but I do know that for well over a minute everyone in the vicinity looked as if they'd been deep frozen, then snapped out of it and carried on with whatever they were doing. I had this horrible sensation that only I knew what was going on; as if a 'freeze ray' had beamed down on everyone, but missed me. I'm glad my wife commented as this showed it wasn't a solus hallucination, heatstroke, or whatever; it's never happened before.

Jack Romano, Worksop, Nottinghamshire, 2007

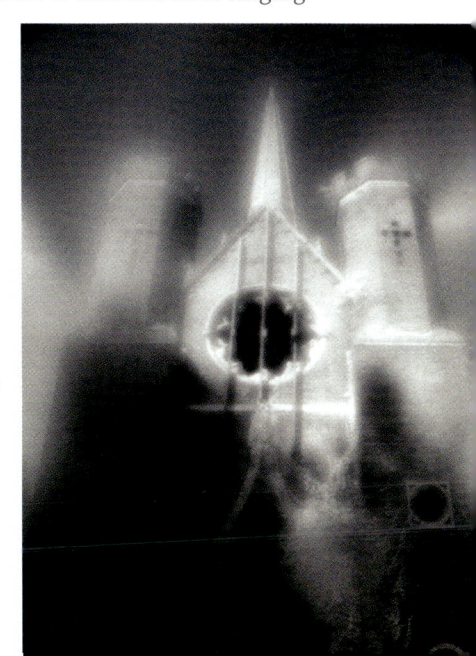

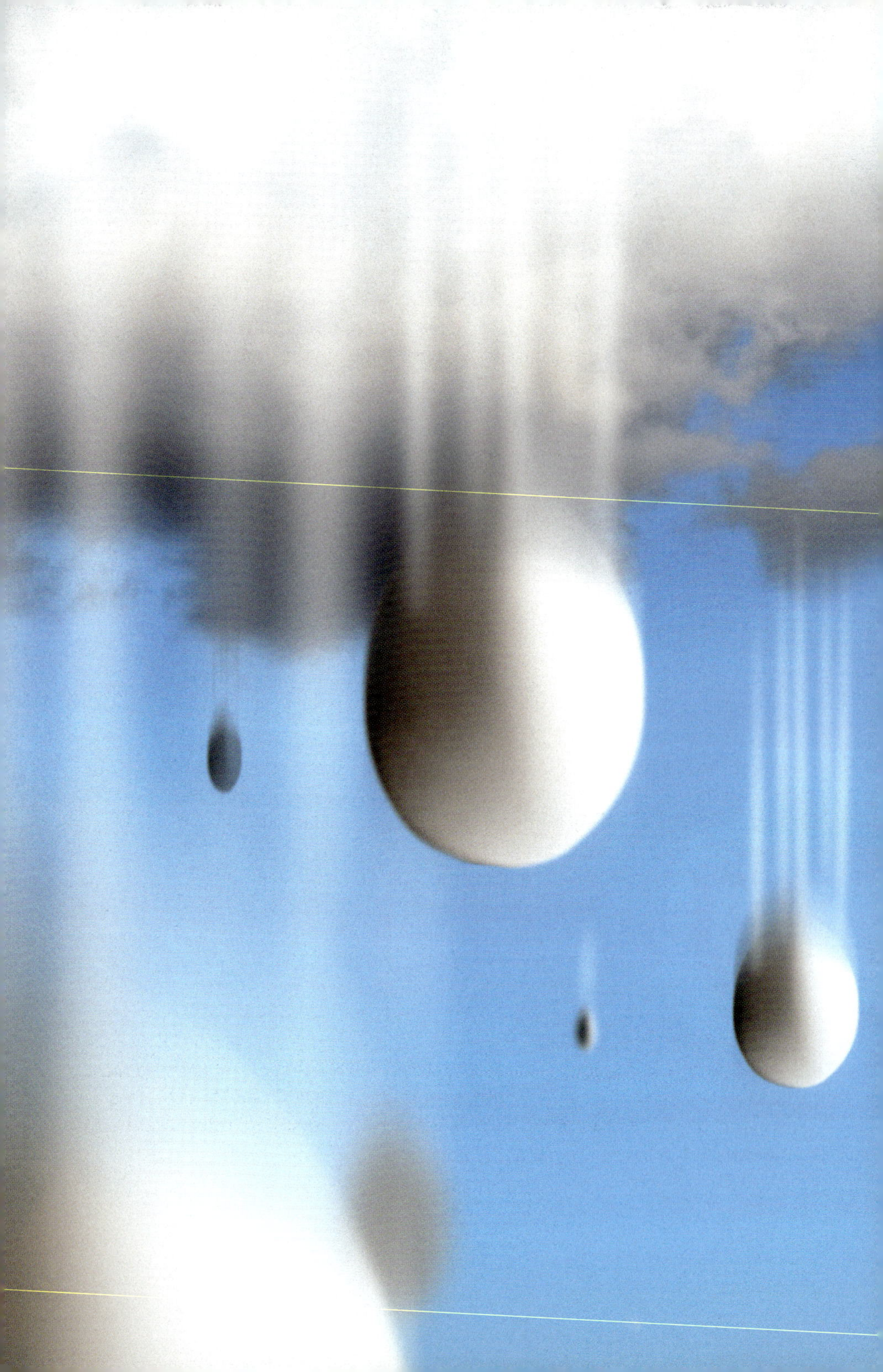

6 *Out Of the Blue*

There was a time when science maintained that reports of stones falling from the sky were folktales. In fact, all manner of things besides meteorites and water bombard the Earth. Zoologist Ivan Sanderson called them 'Fafrotskies' – things that are alleged to have 'fallen from the skies' – and they can include everything from frogs and fish to golfballs, nails and tinsel...

STUFF FROM THE SKY

COSMIC YOKE

One Sunday night at 11.30 in Huddersfield, in (I believe) January 1986, I walked from the railway station to the bus station with a suitcase in one hand and a sports bag in the other. After walking for a few minutes, I saw an old man waiting for a bus outside the Caledonian cafe. It dawned on me that he was the only person I had seen in the town. At a distance of about five metres (16ft) we looked at each other closely. I thought he was going to speak. As I looked into his eyes, an egg (hen's I presume) exploded with extreme force in his face! It was so violent it made a slapping noise and his head was thrown right back. He staggered backward into the cafe windows and almost keeled over. I stood there like a maniac and looked all around. No cars, no people, no sounds, just me, with my hands full, and him. After a few seconds he managed to compose himself and we both looked around for an assailant. I stood rooted to the spot and replayed the scene in my head. The egg seemed to materialise an inch (2.5cm) from his face and hit him with extraordinary force. After checking he still had all his faculties about him, I left.

Rob Kirbyson, Pershore, Worcestershire, 1997

IT HAPPENED TO ME! **OUT OF THE BLUE**

SUNGLASSES FROM HEAVEN
About 11.15 this morning [16 Jan 1986] I parked my car in Conyngham Road, Shepherd's Bush, West London, and crossed the Goldhawk Road to perform an act of honesty – pay £10 to a wine shop that had undercharged me before Christmas. As I came back across the road to my car, I heard a sound of something falling lightly near me and I looked down to see a pair of glasses lying a foot or two away. I bent down to pick them up and looked to see who had dropped them.

The only person nearby was a cyclist who was actually wearing glasses. I asked him if they were his, he denied it and rode away. I saw they were a brand new pair of sunglasses with no scratches. It occurred to me that they might have been thrown from a moving car, but I concluded that this was very unlikely because the sound of them falling was quite gentle, not as of something thrown with force. Nor is there any possibility that they were attached to my clothing as they fell a little distance from me and I was wearing a close-fitting coat with no folds in which they could have become entangled. Was my act of honesty rewarded with this gift? They were just the type I would have chosen for myself!
Margaret Hickey, Chiswick, London, 1986

WATCH OUT BELOW!
At 1am on 18 December 2000 in Tweed Heads, a town in New South Wales close to the border with Queensland, I saw a mango fell from clear skies and land almost at my feet, before bouncing several times across gravel. Closer observation revealed that it was unripe, unpunctured by teeth, and dry, hence unlikely to have been dropped by a flying fox. In any case, there weren't any flying foxes around. The following night, at 10pm, in similar circumstances, another mango fell at my feet, this time on grass. Since I don't like mangoes, is this some sort of cosmic joke? I just hope it's not a phantom greengrocer.
Phillip A Ellis, Tweed Heads, New South Wales, 2000

HOLY MARY!
About five or six years ago, I was visiting my mum's house in Isleworth, Middlesex. I got off the bus onto a wide pavement, quite far from any houses, and no cars were passing. A rosary dropped on me, apparently out of the sky. I looked all around me, but there was no one in sight and the street was completely quiet. I wasn't standing underneath a tree and there were no planes overhead. The event spooked and baffled me, as it still does, but not being religious I don't take it to

OUT OF THE BLUE   IT HAPPENED TO ME...

> *"I was visiting my mum's when a rosary dropped on me, apparently out of the sky"*

be of any great consequence. However, as friends and family think it must have been some kind of 'sign', I keep it just in case.
Nicola Savage, London, 1996

STRANGE SHOWERS

GOLFBALL RAIN?
In April 1975 when tracing a disused footpath I was crossing rough and unfrequented ground about a mile west of Saundersfoot, South Wales, at an altitude of about 150ft (46m), when I noticed a golfball in the grass, and looking around I picked up about a dozen within a small area. I thought at first that the balls might have been lost by a careless and affluent golfer practising, but later I decided that no golfer in his senses would practise on such rough ground when there was a smooth field a few yards away – so returning to the place a few days later and searching more carefully I discovered more balls, making about 30 in all. Many had been trampled into the ground by cows that use the place, and were barely visible, so probably more could have been found by digging. The balls varied from apparently new, clean ones to badly battered; I gave them away to local golfers. The place where I found them is on the side of a valley that slopes at about 30 degrees. It is rectangular, about 50 by 30 yards (46x27m), and is in the corner of a large field, but separated by a hedge with gaps in it. The surrounding

hedges are wide belts of brambles with shrubs and trees. I found no balls outside this area.

I considered the possibility that these balls could have been transported from Tenby golf links, a distance of about three and a quarter miles (5km), by magpies which flock in this area during the spring. Though I have never seen seagulls there, I thought they might have done it. The seagulls around here dig cockles out of the sand, carry them up to a height of about 30ft (9m) and then drop them, causing them to open. I wrote to the Royal Society for the Protection of Birds about this but their reply was that it was unlikely that birds were responsible.

I continued to visit the place during 1975 but found no more balls. Much rain prevented me struggling through mud to reach the site during January and February 1976 but when I got there in early April there was a new supply of balls just as in the previous April – and again I collected about 30. I then looked forward to a regular supply of balls each April but since 1976 I have not found any.
AT Ryland, Saundersfoot, Dyfed, 1981

AN AFRICAN FISH FALL

I was a boy of seven in 1964, and I lived in the Lower Gweru District, not far from Gweru Town [in what was then called Rhodesia]. A friend and I were playing in the rain when to our amazement fish dropped from the sky right in front of our eyes. We actually saw them before they hit the ground. At first we wanted to run into the hut but decided against that, so we took the fish and roasted them.
Elias Paul Mutwira, Zimbabwe, 1990

SHEERWATER FISH FALL

On the morning of Friday 15 January [1993] at around 7:30am I walked to the bottom of my garden in St Michael's Road, Sheerwater, and saw a fish on the path. There were others on the lawn, in the rose bush and on the shed roof, all within a 15ft (4.6m) radius. I counted 12 in all, ranging from four to five inches (10-13cm) and looking like sprats. I couldn't see any in adjacent gardens. The previous night had been very windy and stormy, with winds from the south-west. I contacted the *Woking Review*, which carried a short report on 23 January. Later I heard that John Field, who lives next door but one, had found 11 fish within a small area in his garden. He is a keen fisherman and also thought they looked like sprats, which are of course seawater fish. The sea is almost 40 miles (64km)

away, and the Thames over six miles (9.6km). The fish smelled, so they could have been out of the water a long time.
Derek Gosling, Sheerwater, Surrey, 1993

SNAIL HAIL

The following incident happened when I was a student living in Walthamstow, east London. It was either in the autumn of 1985, or the spring of 1986. I was ringing my mother from an old phone box by the Shern Hall Methodist Church, on the junction of Shernhall Street and Oliver Road. It was early evening, and a light rain began to fall. Suddenly, I heard a knock on the phone box. Assuming it was somebody waiting to use the phone, I turned around, but couldn't see anybody. A few moments later I again heard a knock, but again couldn't see anybody. The knocks continued at intervals of five or 10 minutes, but I didn't pay them much attention.

I was on the phone for about an hour. As I left the phone box I saw that it was covered with snails (I think they were common banded snails). As a life sciences student, I could have taken a specimen home to identify, but I was too unnerved by the whole experience to be thinking logically. There were also snails on the ground in a small area (about one metre in radius) around the telephone box. It looked as if the snails had fallen onto the telephone box and some had crawled away. I couldn't see any other snails in the vicinity. I wonder if the metal phone box had somehow attracted the fall of snails.
Ms KJ Kimberly, Dagenham, Essex, 1996

FROG RAIN

About 30 years ago, in 1976, I witnessed a veritable deluge of frogs. In those days, I used to leave my office in Sydney, Australia, and drive some 125 miles (200km) south to a very small fishing village called Greenwell Point. I used to drive to a town called Nowra, then turn off and follow a narrow road for some nine miles (15km) to Greenwell Point. One day I was late leaving Sydney, and it was around 10 o'clock at night by the time I got to Nowra. It had been raining more or less all the way, but from Nowra on towards Greenwell Point it was heavy driving rain with a lot of leaves and branches over the road. One of my companions remarked that it must be starting to hail, as he could hear something striking the car's roof. A lot of small whitish objects starting to accumulate on the bonnet, but because of the driving rain we couldn't ascertain what they were.

IT HAPPENED TO ME! OUT OF THE BLUE

When we got within a mile of Greenwell Point, the rain slackened off considerably and we were able to see that the road was virtually covered with very small objects, no more than 15 or 20mm long, which appeared whitish in the headlights. We stopped to see what they were, and were astonished to find that all over the road and also on the roof and bonnet of the car were very small frogs, which appeared to be quite well and lively. There were still some falling while we were out of the car. Not long after, the rain stopped falling and so did the frogs.

I can't say that the frogs came from the sky as it was pitch dark, but unless they came from the overhanging trees, there appears to be no other explanation. It was only afterwards that I regretted not keeping one or two for identification. Subsequent conversations with locals seemed to indicate that this had not been witnessed before, and although there were frogs in the area, they were not in the habit of living in trees and in their millions.

Mervyn FW Nightingale, Londonderry, New South Wales, 2006

NEVADA FROG FALL

In August 2006 I was driving east on a hot day across the desert country of eastern Nevada on Highway 50, about 15 miles (24km) outside the town of Eureka. For a half hour or so I had watched the sky to the east darken in front of me until I saw a massive thunderstorm moving from north to south across my path. I have been driving this highway for almost 40 years two or three times a year and often remark that these storms tend to cross the highway coincident with the moment when I pass by them. I was interested to see if that would be the case this time.

I observed the dark thunderhead and its growing sheet of downpour as I came toward it and saw that we would, indeed, collide. The sheets of water did reach the road at about the same time that I reached that point and violently pelted the car, a Jeep Cherokee. I quickly noticed that this was not just rain, but more like hail – but, weirdly, not hail because the drops, sort of white blobs, were not making the metallic sound of rain or hail but were making a soft, thumping sound.

I slowed the car from a speed of about 60 mph (96km/h) to about 25 mph (40km/h) and saw that these were not hailstones but something else. I brought the car to a stop and saw (to my amazement) that the highway, and my hood, were covered with small round toad-like creatures; there must have been many thousands of them, some lying flat on the road and some hopping off toward

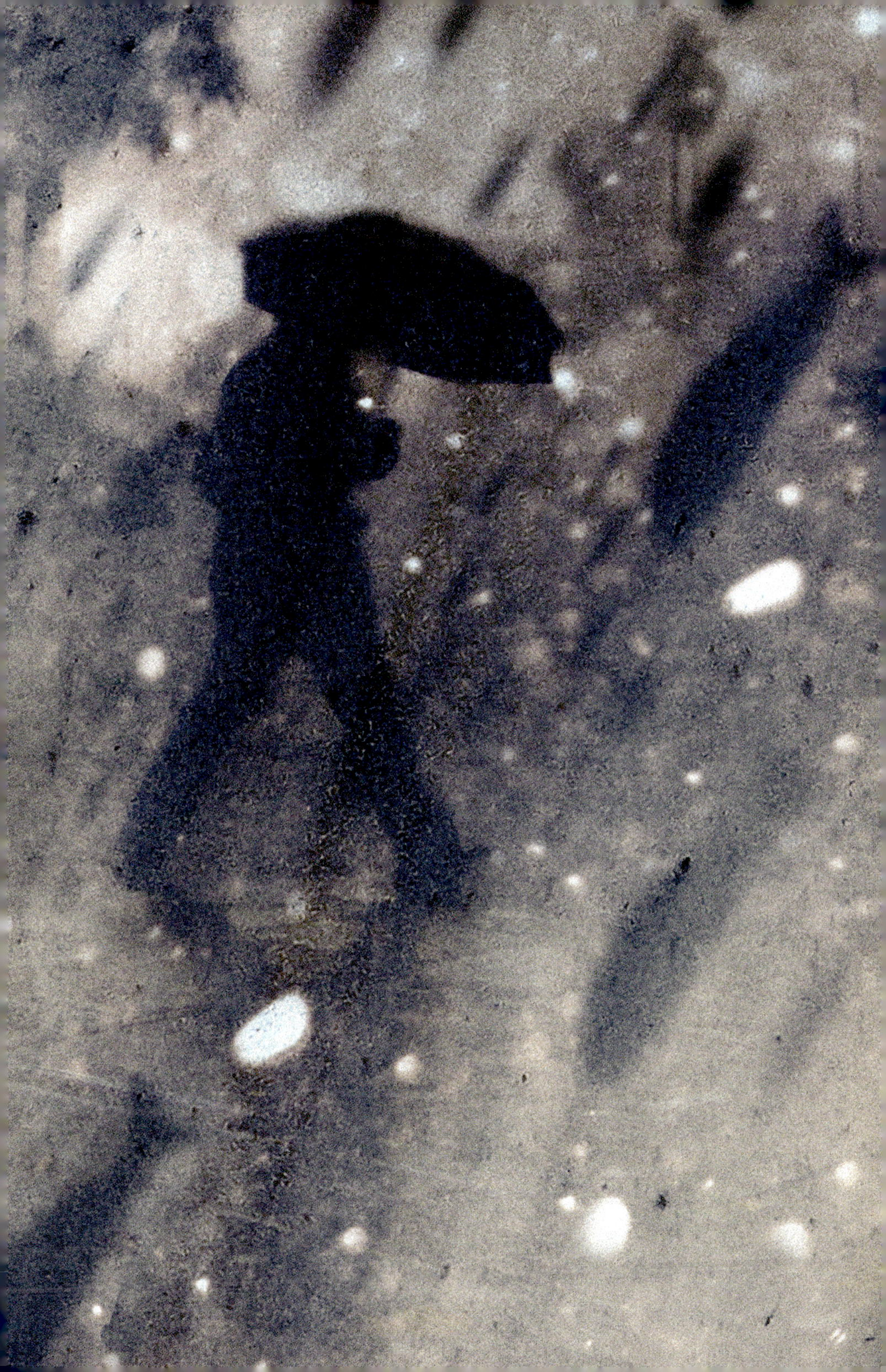

the verges. I got out and confirmed that they were, indeed, toads/frogs, about 1in to 1.25in (2.5-3cm) in diameter, white on the belly and with a sort of silver-tan with light leopard spots on the back. I had a camera, but I couldn't think of how to take a photograph in a way that would make people believe me. I hardly believed it myself. I drove on; still stunned, but wiser.
Wayne Poulsen, by email, 2007

STRAW FALL IN NORFOLK
There was a fall of straw in Sheringham on the north Norfolk coast at 3pm on 27 July 1995. It was witnessed by myself, my wife Gaynor and my eight-year-old daughter Lauren.

It took place in the large car park, approximately 150 by 80 metres (164 by 87 yards), between the main A149 coastal road and the railway station. The fall appeared to be limited to this area, with only a few strands in the road alongside the car park and on the nearby roundabout. Inside the car park, however, it fell in good quantities at a more or less uniform rate, rather like the beginning of a decent snow fall.

By standing underneath it and looking up, I was able to verify that the straw was falling slowly and vertically out of an almost clear blue sky, which had only a few small fluffy white clouds. For the most part the straw was in separate strands with no large tangled mats of vegetation, as there would surely have been had it blown off the back of a lorry.

The latter would seem a likely explanation, except... why did the straw fall in such a localised area, and vertically? Surely a lorry would produce a horizontal trail. In a week's holiday, where we did almost 300 miles (480km)up and down the north Norfolk coast, we didn't see a single lorry with bales of straw or anything similar on the back. In any case, a lorry could not pick up enough speed in such a built-up area, with a roundabout and heavy traffic, to shed its load in such a way.

And why were all the locals taking no notice at all, as if there was a straw fall at 3 o'clock every day in Sheringham?
John Knifton, Nottingham, 1995

IT HAPPENED TO ME...

EXTRAORDINARY DESIGN

Alchemy (England) 1977 gothic

Send for our 64 page catalogue with all our ranges in jewellery, accessories, giftware & T-shirts, including UL13 and AlchemyPoker. Please send your name & address plus a cheque or P.O. for £3 (EUR5.00) payable to: "Alchemy"

Alchemy (FT Year Book 08)
Hazel Drive, Leicester, LE3 2JE
T: 0116 282 4824
F: 0116 282 5352
email: mailorder@alchemygothic.com
Please quote 'FT Year Book 08' when responding to this advert. Trade & wholesale enquiries welcome.
Contact the sales team: Lyn, Georgia, Dan or Sarah
Plus Online ordering at:
www.oldcuriosityshop.net

Laura Knight-Jadczyk
HIGH STRANGENESS

Hyperdimensions and the Process of Alien Abduction.

2nd Edition with preface by Richard M. Dolan.
Coming soon from **www.redpillpress.co.uk**
Call 01225 481635 for a catalogue

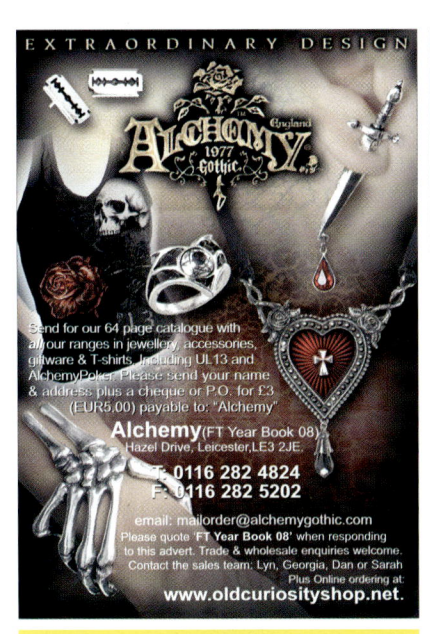

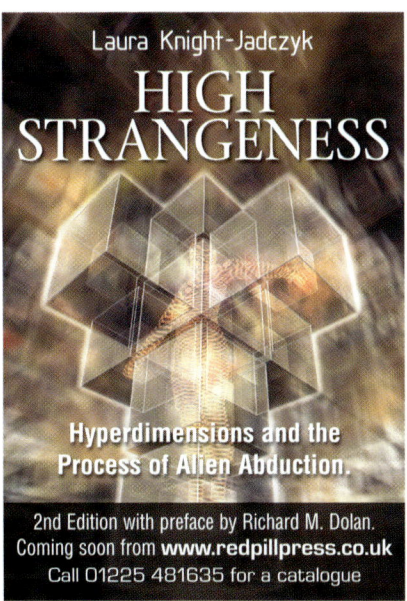

How We Were Made
A book of revelations
by William Neil
This is a much enlarged second edition

"...... Neil demonstrates a host of dazzling numerical correspondences, mostly extrapolated from the famous number 666; multiplied out (6 x 6 x 6), it gives a key number 216, which produces other fundamental constants when it is divided or multiplied. ... Neil applies his findings to show how 666 and related numbers can be found in the human form... in monuments like the Great Pyramid and Stonehenge, in the Earth's position in the solar system, and in ancient and modern measuring systems. It can even be seen in the "building and placing" of the moon. ... If you're fascinated by numbers and sacred geometry, this book will be a treat."

Nexus Magazine review, Aug/Sep 2007

"Highly recommended"
David Icke

Order
this best seller
now!

ISBN 978 0 9545957-1-5

Send a cheque or postal order for £15, with your details, to: Oracle Books. P.O. Box 2467, Reading, England, RG4 7WU
Also from Waterstone's, or any bookshop (£14), and amazon.co.uk

---

NEW AUTHORS

PUBLISH YOUR BOOK
ALL SUBJECTS INVITED

WRITE OR SEND YOUR MANUSCRIPT TO

ATHENA PRESS

QUEEN'S HOUSE,
2 HOLLY ROAD
TWICKENHAM
TW1 4EG

www.athenapress.com
info@athenapress.com

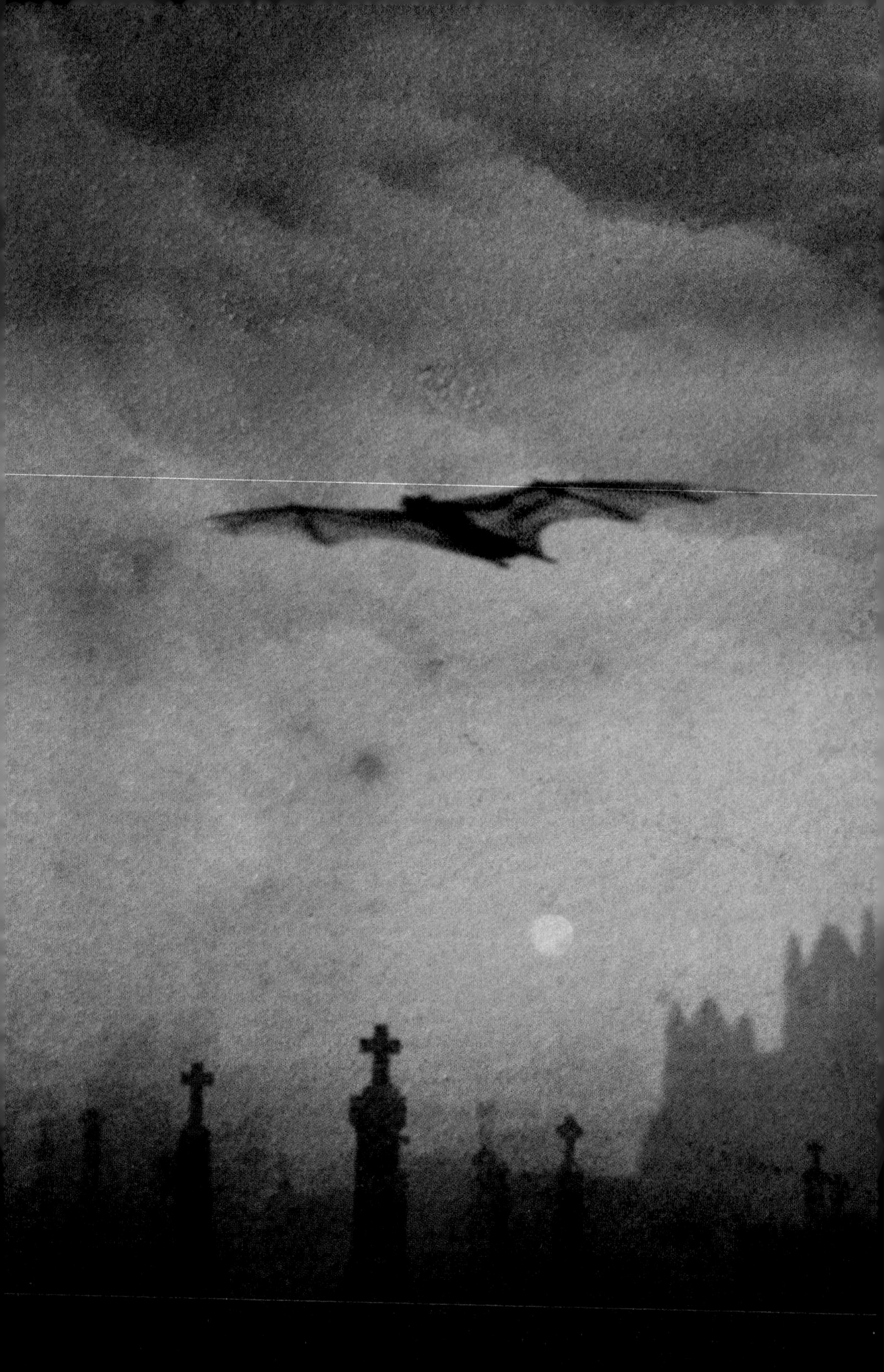

7 Strange Creatures

> Since the days maps bore the legend "here be dragons", man has been fascinated by tales of bizarre beasts. The creatures might resemble mythological monsters – a sea serpent, a birdman, vampire leopards – or be mutant versions of regular members of the animal kingdom, like a winged cat or an alien toilet frog. They might even be otherwordly phantoms, the returning shades of beloved pets...

MYSTERIOUS MONSTERS

MAN-BIRD
In June 1998 I went on a biology field trip to Marlow's Sands in Wales to study the ecology on the local rocky shores with my biology group. While there, some friends and myself walked along the clifftops. One of our friends had stayed behind, so when we saw a large figure standing further along the path we thought it was him, sitting on a stile. That was the point at which it took off and flew over the edge of the cliff. This 'Man-Bird' appeared to be a very large raven, about human size with a fairly wide wingspan. I wondered whether anyone else might have reported seeing the 'Man-Bird' in the area, or if local farmers had been losing lambs?
Simon Clabby, by email, 1999

GIANT BIRD SIGHTING
On 6 July 2000 I was mowing the upper 20 acres of the graveyard where I work in north-western Pennsylvania, Erie County Memorial Gardens. It was about 3pm and I was nearing the edge of 15 undeveloped acres of the cemetery. The graveyard borders hundreds of undeveloped acres of Erie County, and Interstate 90, which runs east to west across the US.

As I cut the lawns I usually absorb the view of the woods as I pass by, and on this occasion I saw something I can't explain. Out from the brush of small trees directly north of the mausoleum a large bird flew into the air. I have seen many large birds in the area, but this one was enormous. As it passed by the high tension wires I estimated that its wingspan was between 15 and 17ft (4.6–5.2m). It was dark grey with little or no neck, and a circle of black under its head. Its beak was very thin and long, about a foot in length.
Robin Swope, by email, 2001

THE CADDINGTON BIRDMAN
In about 1981, when we were children, my sisters, a group of friends and I had a picnic in Bluebell Wood, outside Caddington, near Luton, Bedfordshire. Halfway through the picnic, our friend Gary stood up, stared and pointed. What we saw was a tall (about 8ft/2.4m), dark, brown/black creature. It had red eyes, pointy ears on top of its head and seemed to be a cross between man, bird and bear. It started gliding towards us and seemed to be levitating on a yellow light.

We started to run, and what I remember most was that it seemed impossible to run, almost as if we were being pulled back towards it. We broke out of the wood and into an open cornfield. As we ran across the field, we could see the yellow glow staying within the trees and skirting round the field. It was travelling fast and it was a race between us getting straight across and it going all the way round. We got to the other side and ran through a large tunnel under the M1, leading into Runley Road, Luton. A massive iron grill covered the far end of the tunnel, but there was a gap just big enough for us kids to slip through. We all got through and kept running. But we heard the huge iron grate being shaken behind us and an awful screeching noise, amplified by the tunnel.

I'll never forget how terrifying the whole thing was. The following days we would look out of our bedroom windows over towards Bluebell Wood, because we were convinced the Thing was alien. And yes, two nights later we saw a light zip across the sky and zoom off in a flash.
Colby Pope, London, 2003

THE MONSTER OF DEVIL'S POINT
One Sunday morning in 1987, while I was living in Plymouth, South Devon, a friend came to stay for the weekend and we both went fishing off Devil's Point, a small quay on the Plymouth side of the narrowest point of the river Tamar.

> **It had red eyes and seemed to be a cross between a man, a bird and a bear...**

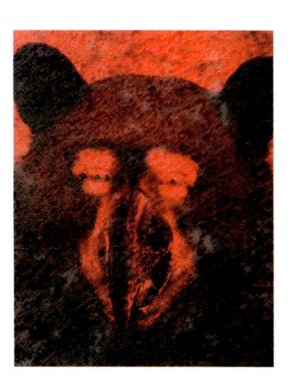

The water here is very deep (130ft/40m) and the current very strong. We had been fishing for about two hours, without much success. It was October, wet and cold. We had been casting out a few yards and letting our lines and bait fall to the bottom of the deep channel.

All we were bringing back up were lumps of strange-looking seaweed that leeched a reddish brown fluid. At one point my friend went back to his car to get two sets of waterproofs. I reeled in another lump of this stuff, rebaited my hook and cast back into the fast flowing, brown water.

I thought I was getting a bite and reeled in expecting to find a small catch on the line. There was nothing. As I removed my tackle from the water I noticed that it was followed up from the depths by the most unusual creature I had ever seen.

A large head popped up out of the water not 10 yards (9m) from me, attached to a neck which rose out of the water by about 3ft (90cm). The head was covered with a fur-like, green-brown skin, had forward facing, dark grey eyes (which looked directly at me) and was similar in shape to that of a very large dog. It was not a seal, animals I have had much contact with as a diver. There were no ears but the top of the head was undulated with a high central ridge. It had a wide mouth and was obviously carnivorous from the shape of the powerful-looking jaw. Its forward facing eyes had fairly heavy brow ridges. From the size of the exposed neck and head, I would estimate the creature to be about twice the size of a horse.

It looked at me for about 15 seconds, submerged vertically and re-emerged slightly closer. It was sizing me up and I think had come to the surface to see what was disturbing it. It remained surfaced for another 5-10 seconds and sank back into the water, leaving circular ripples where it had been. My friend returned shortly afterwards to find me in a very excited state.

I have since learned that the bottom of Devil's Point is home to conger eels, which I believe the creature was hunting at the time. I was previously very sceptical about this 'local myth'. However, I am an experienced scuba diver and have a good knowledge of sea-life. This was most definitely an unidentified species, large and intelligent. I would suggest that anyone doing serious research into this might have a chance of a sighting around conger grounds. How about using a large cageful as bait?

Nic Johnson, by email, 2002

SINGAPORE SERPENT

I once saw a sea serpent in the well-used shipping lane at the back of Singapore Island. We were rounding Changi Point, only about half a mile (0.8km) from the shore, entering the Jahore Straits for the run up to Sembawang Dockyard.

I was leaning against the rail, scanning the shore through a good pair of binoculars. There were two or three people on the beach looking out to sea, or at us, or whatever, when I spotted a grey-black, sinuous body, about one foot (30cm) thick, with the conventional sea serpent humps, undulating through the water only about 150 yards (137m) away in a flat sea. I saw no head, only a series of grey-black humps, and I watched it for at least half a minute, as we passed by at 11 knots. Then it quietly slipped below the surface and disappeared.

By the time I looked around for someone else to confirm the sighting, the 'monster' had disappeared. I had an excellent view through binoculars; it was mid-morning and the bar had not yet opened. I am inclined to think that the people on the shore were also gazing out at something strange.

I wondered how I could fabricate such a 'monster' should I wish to deceive the guileless. The RAF still had a base at Changi, and I wouldn't put it past some of those jokers. But I never talk about it. After all, there are no such things as sea serpents, are there?

S J Adams, Bath, Avon, 2001

GIANT ORANGE SLUG

In the summer of 1984, I was 11, and due to start secondary school that September. I lived in the Hardenhuish area of Chippenham, Wiltshire. I was good friends with two brothers, roughly my age, who lived in a nearby street. One afternoon in late July/August, while exploring the woods behind St Nicholas Church off Hardenhuish Lane, we stumbled on a creature in the grass which scared the holy bejesus out of us. It looked like a bright orange slug with a frilled underside. It was about 2ft (60cm) long and had antennae of a similar length. It was alive, and vibrated, making a soft, snuffling sound. The three of us ran off to tell the nearest adult about our find. My last memory of the day was of seeing my friends' father storm out of his garage towards the woods, with a shovel over his shoulder. Whether he found anything or not, I have no idea.

Sometimes I wonder whether what we saw was a manifestation of our hopes and fears: Big School looming in the autumn, Cold War / mushroom cloud paranoia on the TV all the time and too much time watching *Return of the Jedi*.
Steve Uzzell, Hove, East Sussex, 2005

VAMPIRE LEOPARDS?

Around 1976, I was living in Nairobi, Kenya, in a suburb called Kileleshwa. It was only about three miles (4.8km) out of the centre of town, but bordered by valleys on either side that ranged from a couple of hundred yards to half a mile wide of uncultivated bush and extended at least five miles (8km).

At some point, the neighbourhood dogs, many of which roamed freely around the area, started howling during the night. This was enough to make our own dog want to join them, and he would scratch at the door until he was let out. Throughout the night we would hear the howling at different locations around the neighbourhood, but everyone seemed prepared to put up with the noise, expecting the cause of it to end soon and the dogs to get back to normal.

One day I was told that a dog had died on one of the roads. This wasn't unusual, but what was strange was the lack of blood. I was then told that another dog had died within the previous few days. These deaths were put down to the dogs fighting overnight, hence the howling. However, over the next week or so, the situation stayed the same, dogs out every night howling, and two more dogs found dead. The "dogs fighting overnight" explanation now seemed unlikely, as the same dogs got on well during the day. People started becoming concerned that something else was happening. Finally, some of the local people opened up to me, and told me that in some African cultures, the dog is the biggest enemy of the leopard and that the scent of the leopard is enough to send dogs wild. I was also told that when a leopard grows old, it kills a dog and drinks its blood to rejuvenate! The people who told me this were workers on the lower end of the social scale, largely untouched by Western films or books, and so were very unlikely to have heard or been interested in Western stories of vampires.

Now, at the age of 16, try telling your parents that your pet dog shouldn't go outside because of vampire leopards! So one evening the howling started and our dog went out. In the morning, our house servant told my mother that overnight he had heard an animal in pain in the rear garden where we grew maize. He had opened the door from his small house and the noise had stopped, but feeling the hairs on the back of his neck rising, he didn't want to venture out in the dark without a light. He now planned to investigate but wanted to be accompanied. We found our dog where he had heard the disturbance. Dead. The maize was flattened around it and the fence had been damaged. The dog had two wounds, one on its shoulder, which appeared like a bite mark, the other a big hole in its chest, about 5in (13cm) deep where its heart had been. Had been, because the heart was gone, and in spite of whatever had happened, there were no blood stains on the soil around the dog. I also found large paw prints in the soil, around the size of a large dog's, but without the expected claws at the front.

During the next week or so, a couple more dogs were killed. My mother spoke with the Wildlife Game Department, who confirmed that two leopards that had been in the Nairobi National Wildlife Park could no longer be found, but they were not unduly concerned, and without any sighting of a leopard in the suburbs, could not take any action.

The deaths, and the howling, stopped as suddenly as they had started.
Martin Nield, by email, 2004

ANIMAL GHOSTS

MEWLING MYSTERY
My parents live in an old farmhouse which they spent a number of years renovating. While doing this they found a number of things under the floorboards and in the wall cavities – including, in a space in the attic, a small mummified cat. (It

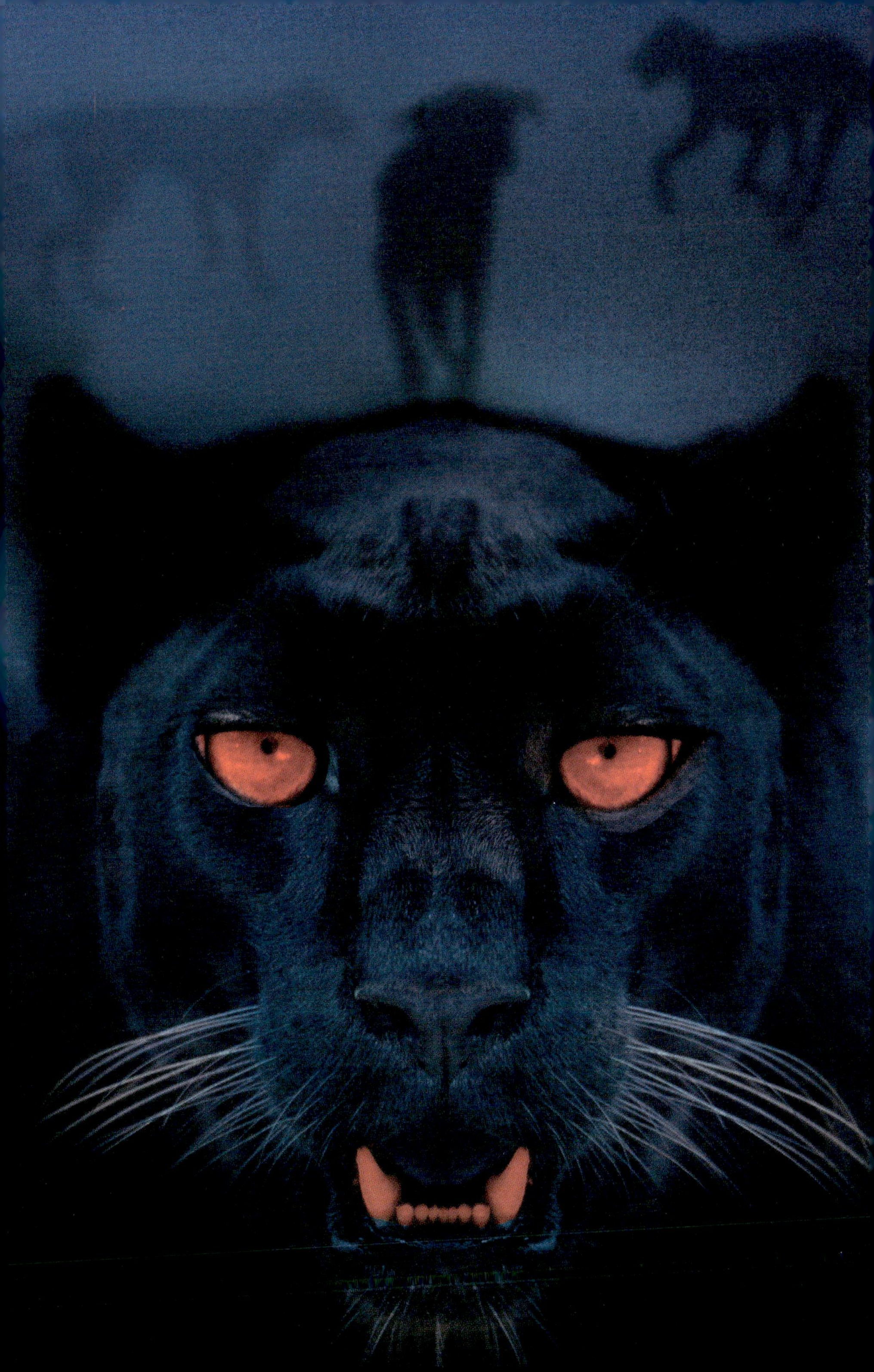

appeared to have crawled in rather than having been put there deliberately.) It was completely dried out and they put it in a box for safekeeping while they decided what to do with it.

My grandmother came over for a visit sometime afterwards and my mother took her on a guided tour of the house. "Oh," my grandmother said as she went into a room full of boxes and clutter, "you never said you'd got a cat!"

"We haven't," replied my mother, puzzled.

"Of course you have. I can hear it purring."

My mother told my grandmother that she must be mistaken and they carried on looking at the rest of the house. The mummified cat's remains were boxed up in that room out of sight, and my grandmother knew nothing about them or the fact that we buried them shortly afterwards.

Emma Cannell, Norwich, Norfolk, 1997

SPECTRAL CAT AND PHANTOM PONY

About 12 months ago we had our cat put down after a long illness. He was a major character and well loved by many people. After a few days, I began to see him around the house again, coming into rooms as I arrived home. This reached the pitch that he would come in through the cat flap while I was having breakfast, with the cat flap moving as he came in. There was no mistaking this cat – there cannot be many of his colour with one eye and a plastic hip.

A number of years ago, I was cycling down a sunken lane after leaving a friend's house near the Stiperstones in Shropshire in the early hours. A large white pony came over the hedge from my right, landed on the road and just disappeared. It was as if there was a screen halfway across the road; the animal vanished slowly from head to tail. This was incredibly vivid and real; I was used to working with horses at the time.

Phillip Evans, by email, 1999

THE RETURN OF WELLINGTON

I am a home-visiting private tutor of music. About seven years ago, I began teaching electronic organ to Ian, a retired police officer. In the course of the fifth weekly visit and while listening to Ian's organ work, my attention was drawn to the door in front of me, which on this day was ajar by about 8in (20cm). A large white and tan cat was slowly walking through the gap. Somehow, I hadn't noticed it pass my chair. Recalling that my pupil had previously said he owned a cat and

STRANGE CREATURES **IT HAPPENED TO ME!**

> ❝ It was a large white pony that vanished slowly from head to tail… ❞

that it was incontinent, I followed it immediately, at the same time explaining my actions to him. The room was, in fact, a tiny closet with toilet facilities. There was no other door, no sign of the cat and no way it could have doubled back past me. I came out from the closet.

My host had run from the room, but returned promptly, holding a black cat. "I thought you were mistaken," he said. "I knew the cat was asleep in the other room". "The cat I saw was white and tan," I said, "not black". His reaction to this observation was startling. He dropped the cat, and clasped his hands together. "Thank God!" he positively shouted, "Now I know I'm not insane! What you saw was my old cat, Wellington. He died six years ago and is buried outside. Since he died, I have seen him and felt him brush against me on many occasions. My wife thinks I'm mad. My son thinks I'm mad. Oh, thank you so much!"

Roy C Cotterill, Orrell, Lancashire, 2003

HIDING FROM THE DOG

In 1933, when I was eight, I lived in Woodseats, Sheffield, with my parents, three sisters, and a cat. I was pestering my father for a dog. I shared a double bed with two of my sisters, aged 19 and 16; the eldest, aged 20, had a small bedroom to herself.

I was put to bed before my sisters. Every night a large dog walked from the door, round the bed to a certain spot. I don't know what happened then, as I shot under the hot and stuffy bedclothes as far as I could go; there to sleep until, I suppose, I was pulled up by my sisters. I knew the dog was large by the sound of its step on the lino and I had no doubt that it was black. Wanting to own a dog was one thing, but this creature frightened me. We hadn't got a dog!

When my eldest sister left home, I was put into the small bedroom. One morning, my mother asked me if I had heard the hullabaloo from my sisters' room in the night: "They were screaming blue murder... they said there was a horrible noise coming out of the picture." This was a sketch of Colyton Church in Devon by my 19-year-old sister. I told her I had heard nothing. She asked if I had ever heard anything when I slept there; and, to my lasting shame, I said "No" and left the room swiftly. I feared being laughed at if I had mentioned the dog.

Sheila Clark, Wraysbury, Buckinghamshire, 1999

MUTANTS

FROGGY OMEN

I live in a ground floor flat in Birmingham. One morning, I raised the seat on my toilet and noticed something projecting from under the rim of the bowl. At first I took it for one of those sticky blooms you get on rhododendrons. However, a closer inspection determined that the object was a small frog. My first response was to scoop the little blighter out and return him to the wild via the toilet window, but innate paranoia stayed my hand. The frog was of a colour I call premature-baby pink, an unpleasant fleshy purple; not a normal-looking froggy colour at all. It brought to mind images of poisonous tree-frogs of the Amazon basin (rather than the Birmingham toilet bowl); I could almost hear the hushed tones of David Attenborough describing the little critter's toxic nature. So, rather than risk an appearance in *FT's* 'Strange Deaths' column, I flushed the Alien Toilet Frog (ATF) away; it took two goes to swish him around the u-bend.

My own ATF theories are as follows: it was an exotic variety, escaped from a private collection or travelling show; or a normal frog whose famously sensitive skin had been effected by a cocktail of bleaches and detergents; or, perhaps, a representative of some weird, mutant breed of urban sewer-dwelling frog; or, finally, an omen of ill luck, presaging some unutterable doom which has yet to overwhelm me.

What really struck me about this encounter with the supernormal was the way it undermined my composure. For several days I felt as if I were walking on thin ice; as if reality were hollow and eggshell-thin. All this from meeting one little

ATF; no wonder people who suppose themselves to have encountered Bigfoot, ghosts or aliens seem a little strung out.
Euan Smith, Acocks Green, Birmingham, 2000

ALBINO LOBSTERS

I live in a terraced house in Kentish Town, north London. Some while back, over a period of months, I found what appeared to be lobsters in my garden. They were quite large and albino. No one believed me, and I didn't think to keep them – they weren't too fresh. One night, a friend who was visiting for dinner stumbled upon one of these creatures by my back door. We concocted a number of implausible theories for their presence, including seagulls snatching them from market stalls.

Finally, he posted the specimen to the Natural History Museum, where the Crustacea Section was able to help. The aggressive Turkish Crayfish (*Astacus leptodactylus salinus*) have turned up in Camden's canal system. The road next to my own is called Angler's Lane. The river for which this road was named went underground long ago, but still links up with the drains between my road and the canal. The crayfish appear to have crawled out of my drainage outlet and onto the lawn. I am now beginning to appreciate the thin line between the commonplace and the absurd…
Christopher Fowler, Kentish Town, 1993

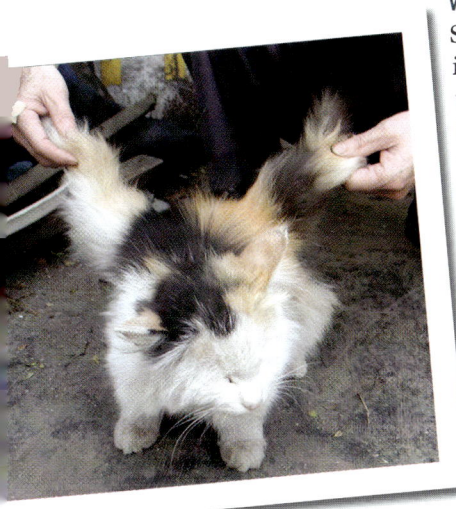

WINGED CATS

Saturday, 23 May 1998 was hot and sunny here in Kumamoto, Kyushu, Japan, and I waited for the cool of night to go running. At midnight I ran my usual, familiar route. Halfway through, I came across a couple of cats sitting on a wall overlooking the road. I called to them as I would to any cats. As I am unable to call cats in Japanese, they don't usually respond to my miaowing and pusspussing noises, but this time one of them did.

It jumped up and purringly made its way over to me. I was shocked to feel how bumpy its back was; then I realised that

IT HAPPENED TO ME! STRANGE CREATURES

it had weird growths – not fat or bones, but jutting out fur-covered wing-like growths. I looked the cat over and in all other respects it seemed quite normal. Admittedly it was dark, but a little light was coming from an overhead lamp and I have no doubt about what I saw. The growths were triangular in shape and covered in soft fluffy fur. They felt like the wings of a chicken, although they were not so long. I stroked it a little longer and then ran on.
Rebecca Hough, Kumamoto. Japan, 1998

Back in 1975 my neighbourhood was on the edge of what was once one of Arizona's last true wilderness areas; now it's tract houses and luxury retirement golf communities. One of the original residents was an elderly widow with about a hundred cats, all descended from a single pair. Of course, by that time the generations were inbred as all hell, and bore little resemblance to average cats. The woman died suddenly, and the folks who dealt with her estate handled the cats in a quick manner — they opened all the doors and windows and shoo'd them away. We were soon overrun with cats. Coyotes, foxes and golden eagles soon took care of the majority, and neighbours armed with .22 rifles took care of the rest.

One cat was left. I first noticed this strange beast at a distance, a small bluish feline with what looked like a pair of large wings hanging off the top of its rear pelvis. It had a face that looked like it had been hit by a brick, flat and grossly distorted. One eye was clearly larger than the other, and one side of the jaw had no lip covering. It looked quite ghastly, really. This cat seemed to take delight in killing all manner of native small wildlife and not eating them, and raiding local gardens with the sole purpose of smashing and trashing anything that grew. It got into my small garden twice in early summer, completely destroying it.

Once I watched this animal from a few feet away before it noticed me. It was thin, starving, deformed in face and body, and was covered with tics, lice and all manner of clinging insects. The 'wings' caught my attention. The two hanging off the pelvis were about 6in (15cm) long, 2in (5cm) wide at the base, perhaps an inch (2.5cm) wide at the end, and were covered with dirty fur. The cat saw me, drew back as if to attack, and the wings began to flail around in random directions. Then I noticed two deformed claws sticking out of the end of each tip. The cat let out a fearful scream and fled faster than I thought possible. When it turned, I noticed a second set of wings, much smaller than the first, stationary, on top of the creature's shoulders.
Russ Williams, Prescott, Arizona, 1999

SUBSCRIPTION OFFER

ONLY £1

3 ISSUES OF FORTEAN TIMES FOR JUST £1

PLUS! GET A FREE FORTEAN TIMES MUG

From folklore and myth to news stories and firsthand sightings, some things simply defy rational explanation. Tracking these phenomena and uncovering the oddities of our mad planet is the mission of only one magazine: Fortean Times.

YOUR PHENOMENAL OFFER:
- **3 issues** for £1 to start your subscription – if you're not completely satisfied, simply cancel and pay no more than £1
- **FREE** Fortean Times mug
- **SAVE up to 29%** on the shop price if you continue your subscription
- **FREE delivery to your door** before the issue hits the shops

CALL
0844 844 0049

Or order online at
www.dennismags.co.uk/forteantimes
using offer code GO810BKZ

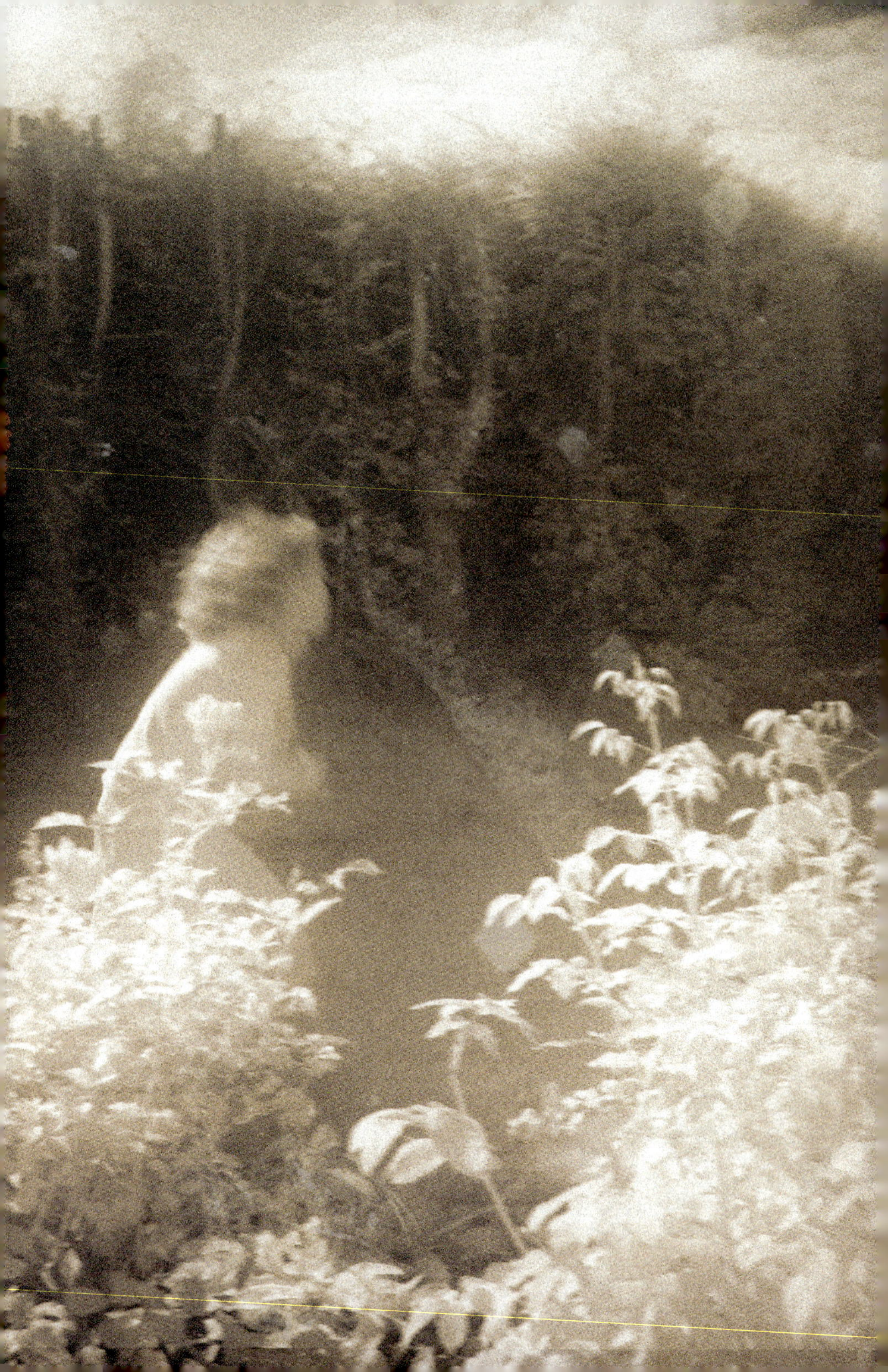

8 The Little People

Legions of little people populate folklore – elves, pixies, sprites, gnomes, dwarves, fairies. Generally, they hide from humans, but occasionally a brownie is heard making shoes or a fairy sighing; a pixie is glimpsed running through woodland, or the shadows of tiny dancers play over a cupboard. Sometimes even the more exotic species – miniature golfers, and flying Barbie dolls – are spotted...

NOISES OFF

KNOCK KNOCK, WHO'S THERE?

Until 1939, when I was 10, my family and I lived in a Victorian terrace in Stewkley, near Leighton Buzzard, Bedfordshire, before moving to my present address in the same village. Opposite the terrace (now demolished) was – and still is – a large house with grounds. The field separating the house from the road was laid out as a small 'gentleman's park' with clumps of trees of various sorts.

One evening – it must have been autumn or winter because it was dark – there came the sound of hammering from high up a pine tree: three hits, hammer laid down, three more hits, and so on. My father mended shoes, so I know what it sounded like.

All the inhabitants of the terrace were out listening – the people from the big house and their servants and probably others as well. The owner of the big house shone a torch up the tree and called out: "Who's there? What are you doing? Stop it!" and things like that, but the sounds continued. They occasionally stopped briefly and then began again. My parents said it lasted for over an hour; to me as a child, it seemed much longer. Then it ceased and, as far as I'm aware, never came again, but as I say we moved, so I can't be sure.

A year or two ago, I met a woman who was something of an expert on folklore.

I told her about the hammering and she said it was a working Brownie, a fairy shoemaker. "There are a lot of reports of that sort of thing," she said. I've never believed in fairies, but it couldn't have been somebody doing it for a joke: what, up a *pine* tree in the dark? There were plenty of other trees easier to climb – beech, lime, horse chestnut. And at that date it couldn't have been a tape recording. Moaning and howling round haystacks in a bedsheet to scare folk, that would be the peak of invention in a village before the war.
Mr J Keen, Leighton Buzzard, Bedfordshire, 1999

FEAR THE FAERIES

My new wife and I went to Aberfoyle, Scotland, in September 1979 to investigate the famous disappearing Reverend Kirk, the 17th century author of *The Secret Commonwealth*, that great book about the faerie folk. At the tourist kiosk in the town centre, we were told that no one in the town believed in Kirk's story any more, nor that the hill behind the town, allegedly housing the hidden gateways to the Faerie lands, was anything more than just a hill. It was thickly covered with trees, with a large oak at the top standing higher than all the rest.

Tradition had it that if you climb the hill at around midnight, on certain nights of the year, the doorways to Faerieland would be visible and open for a man to step through. As we walked up the wide road that curved towards the top of the hill, we realised that this was not a trip to make late at night. The sun was shining, there were birds singing in the trees, yet there was something vaguely unsettling about the area. Even encountering other hikers did nothing to dispel our unease. One expected to be suddenly startled by something otherworldly. I picked up a large branch to use as a walking stick in order to stiffen my resolve to get to the top.

As we climbed, we noticed a faint sound that was becoming louder and louder. It was like thousands of houseflies buzzing all at once. The sound was everywhere and yet its source could not be located. There were no insects in the air or anywhere else on the hill. By this time, nearing the summit, birds had ceased to sing, the air was still and oppressive, and yet was filled with the infernal buzzing. As the noise was permeating everything, even into our skulls, we became even more uncomfortable, and so turned around and walked briskly down the hill.

By the time we reached the bottom, the sound was completely gone. As we crossed the threshold from the hill path to the road back to town, I felt a sudden blow on my right shoulder, immediately causing numbness and tingling in my

> *If you climb the hill at midnight the doorways to Faerieland will be visible*

hand. It did not subside until I had thrown the walking stick back onto the path up Faerie Hill. "What's theirs, they keep..."
Peter Sutherland, by email, 2001

FAIRY HELP
Today is 30 April 2006, Walpurgis Night, and I had an interesting experience this afternoon.

In 1996, I had three experiences over a 48-hour period while travelling through upper New York State, experiences which I can only define as evidence of the existence of fairies. Since that time, I've studied fairly lore in depth and have become something of a believer, though I maintain an open mind on the subject.

I live in Bayridge, Brooklyn; there is a beautiful four-acre botanical garden right on the harbour several long blocks from my home. There are several hawthorn trees on the green, which I know are considered sacred to fairies in some quarters; and I do think of them that way myself. For the last eight years, I've taken a thorn from one of the trees every 31 October and 30 May, and placed it in one of the inner pockets of my wallet; I always place it in the same spot. At the same time, I remove the thorn I've been carrying for half a year, and push it back into the earth beneath the tree I've taken it from. I do this to both honour the fairies and also as a means of seeking a kind of protection from them.

This afternoon, I walked to the botanical garden, sat beneath my favourite hawthorn and searched my wallet for the thorn, but couldn't find it. I removed the entire contents of my wallet and checked every fold: no thorn. But I did notice immediately that my credit card was missing from the pocket where I always keep it by itself. I panicked for a moment, then realised I must have left it at the restaurant where I had dinner the previous evening. I immediately walked back to the diner, and when I entered, the owner smiled, waved, and produced my credit card, which I've never lost or left behind anywhere before.

Back under the hawthorn, I removed a thorn from the tree and placed it in my wallet, thanking the fairies for it as I did so. After a moment, I realised that had the thorn I removed from the tree last October not been missing, I probably wouldn't have discovered my credit card was missing for several more days. Coincidence, personal fancy, or a blessing from the fairies on the afternoon of Walpurgis Night? I am single, and though I share my home with a family member, I'm certain no one goes through my wallet. What actually happened to the missing thorn will probably remain a mystery.
Joseph E Barnes, New York 2006

WOODLAND SIGH

Back in 1986, three friends and I formed a secret society, partly out of dissatisfaction with 1980s youth culture, but mainly for a laugh. This involved spending a lot of time in nearby local woodlands and fields, practising our survival skills, building camps and reciting Monty Python sketches. Around sunset on Midsummer Night's Eve (24 June 1987), from our camp in the woods adjoining a field, we noticed a dog-walker – not unusual, as it was a popular dog-walking spot. However, this one didn't seem normal as the dog was white and the owner was dressed entirely in white, including his hat. Two of my friends decided to try and get a closer look and stalked around the field perimeter, while the other friend and I remained hidden in the bushes to see if the strange-looking character passed us by.

After about five minutes of sitting in silence we heard an unmistakably human sigh directly behind us. But there was no one to be seen, either on the ground or in a tree. We were surrounded in all directions by crisp leaves, so no one could have crept up on us. The noise we heard was like a sigh made by a young woman or a boy and sounded as if it came from someone sitting right there with us. The friend who had been with me recalled the story only last week [July 2007]. He is now a police officer and probably not keen to reveal his identity – but is still adamant concerning what we heard. I'm not sure if it was a faerie, but it was dusk on Midsummer Night's Eve at a place with a pagan history – surely a recipe for faeries!

As for the mysterious dog-walker, he never passed us and the others 'lost' him as they were trying to get closer. He may have been of this world, but the sigh was not.

Chris Kershaw, by email, 2007

I CAN SEE YOU!

SEEING A PIXIE?

At about 3.30 on a late autumn day, my wife and I were out walking the dog near Stourport on Severn. As the light was fading, we decided to take a shortcut home along a disused rail track, overgrown with silver birch. Suddenly my wife looked to her left and said "S--t, what the hell was that!?" I caught a glimpse of an upright two-legged creature about 3-4ft (90-120cm) tall running across the path about 12ft (3.3m) away and disappearing into the trees. It had the appearance of a child, but its head was too large for its body. It moved as fast as a cat running at speed.

I had an overwhelming urge to get as far away as possible, a feeling that I wasn't supposed to bear witness to what I had seen. I legged it, calling to my wife, "Just keep running!" The sketch of the creature below is an accurate image burned into my memory.

Amos, Stourport on Severn, Hereford and Worcester 1998

THE MINIGOLFERS

One evening during May 1994, I was walking home from Askham Bog nature reserve, across Pike Hills golf course, near York. The sun was still shining behind me, so visibility

Sketch of best glimpse of creature I had!

was reasonably good. My attention was drawn to some figures roughly 100 yards (90m) ahead of me, apparently putting a ball around on an otherwise deserted golf course. There were five or six very small figures, which I presumed to be children, quite engrossed in their game. When I was about 50 yards (45m) away, they appeared to become aware of me and I could see that they were not children but very small adults, about 4ft (1m) tall. At this moment one of them appeared to prepare to strike the ball hard in my direction. I ducked behind a nearby tree for a few seconds. When I looked again, the green and fairway were empty. They couldn't have run away in so short a time and my search of the nearby area revealed no sign of them.
J Bardet, by email, 2002

CUPBOARD DANCERS
One night when I was about nine, I was lying in bed with the lights off, wide awake with my bedroom door open and the landing light shining directly on to my bedroom built-in wardrobes. The landing light had a solid glass, translucent, non-patterned shade. A movement on the top cupboard of the right wardrobe caught my eye and when I looked I saw the shadows of four very thin, small people dancing. They were like stick men but one of them had a bushy hair-do. I was fascinated, not scared, and thought it was funny. I must have watched for about 10 minutes as they did what looked like dances from the 1950s. Then curiosity got the better of me, so I got out of bed and had a look out my bedroom door to see what was going on. The landing didn't have any windows as it was a terraced house; it was just walls, the stair banister and the light and there was nothing out there which could explain the shadows. When I looked back at the cupboard the dancers had gone and I never saw them again, but it did seem as though they had had a good time on my cupboard.
SW, Sydney, Australia, 2003

PICCADILLY ELF
I saw an 'elf' in broad daylight and in a crowded, public place. He was of average height and looked solid and physical enough; he certainly didn't have to be coaxed out of the twilight by the exercise of night vision.

It was in September 2000 and I was on a First Aid training course in Bolton. A small number of us were determined to make the most of a week's break from the nine-to-five and we were enjoying ourselves. On the Thursday, however, I

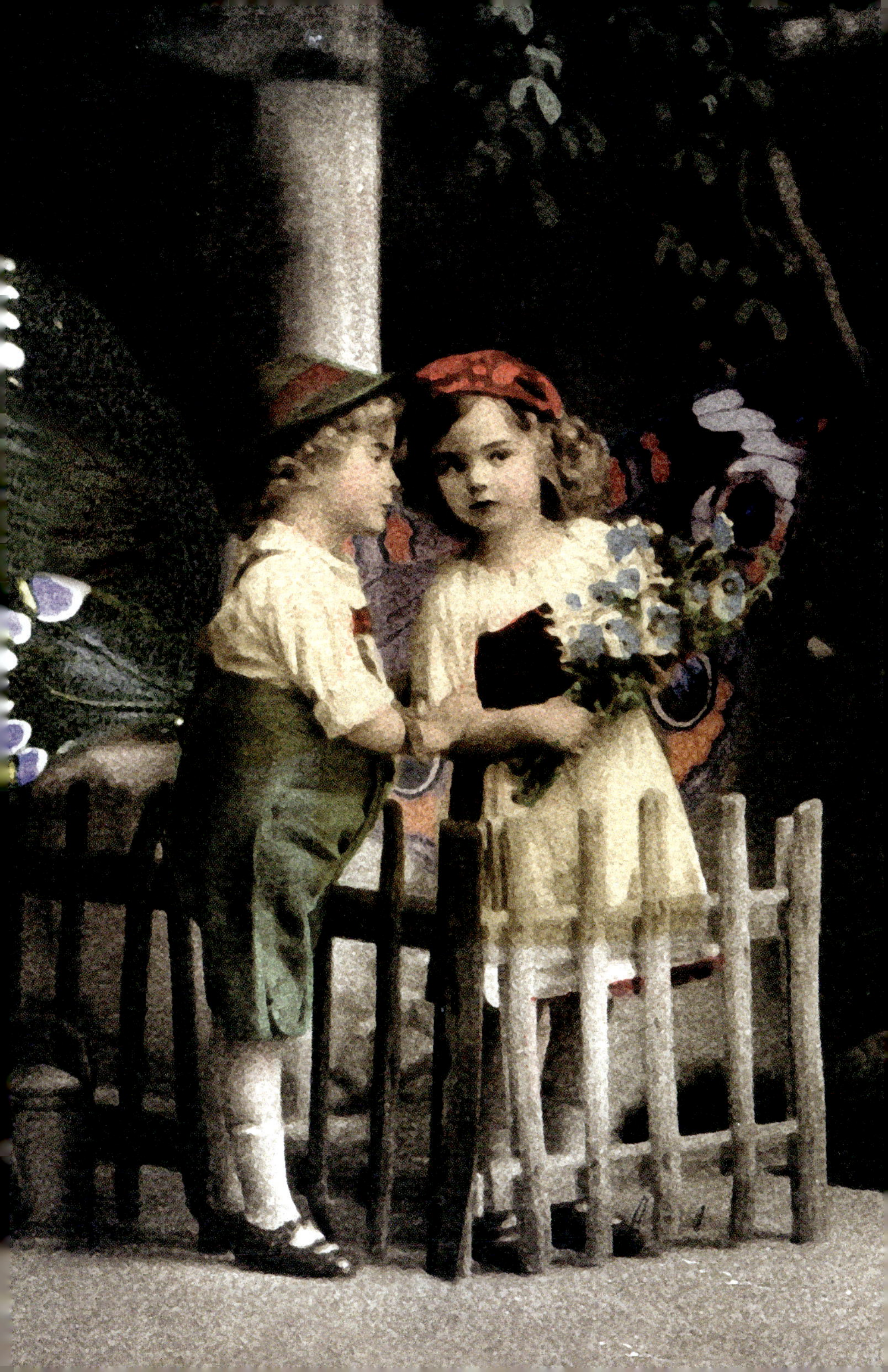

> **" They were in no way remarkable except that one of the men had pointed ears "**

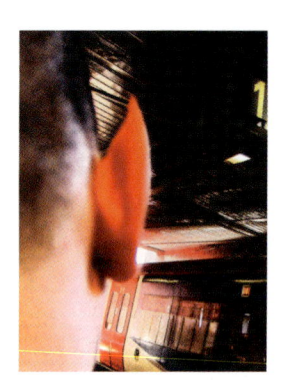

started to realise that, for me, something other than ordinary high spirits had started to prevail. I began to experience the kind of manic euphoria that in the past had acted as a precursor to odd events. I managed to keep a lid on things during the day, but the optimistic, immensely expansive frame of mind reasserted itself during the journey home. It persisted as I changed trains at Manchester Piccadilly and boarded one bound for Stockport.

As I sat idly gazing out of the window, a train pulled in on the opposite platform, and three young men got off. They were dressed in the usual student attire, and were in no way remarkable, except that, as I suddenly realised, one of them had pointed ears. This was an absolute certainty: the ears were far larger than normal, their tops slanting upward and backward to an unmistakable point.

Although accustomed to having the occasional odd experience, I still doubted the evidence of my senses. I glanced surreptitiously at the woman facing me, who was also looking in their direction, but saw no reaction on her part. It was the evening rush hour and the platform was crowded, but the sight failed to evince any kind of response from passers-by.

I then wondered if it could be a practical joke of some kind; but if it was, there was none of the smirking or nudging you might have expected from the lads themselves. They seemed to be deep in conversation, oblivious of anyone around them. The only feeling I had about them was that they had travelled a long way and still had a long way to go.

The event had all the hallmarks of strangeness, incongruity and apparent inconsequentiality that I have come to associate with experiences of this kind. There is never any explanation: to label them may satisfy our need to account for anomalies and dispose of them tidily, but achieves little apart from providing a bogus sense of security.

However, it has made me wonder why it is that elves, fairies, goblins, aliens, etc are so frequently depicted with pointed ears. According to the writer Stan Gooch, the original 'Little People' were our Neanderthal ancestors (or cousins). He suggests that these earlier, 'alternative' humans were mostly nocturnal; their large (and, Gooch argues, possibly pointed) ears a natural adaptation to the environment. A template still much in use – witness its recent reappearance in the Ring Trilogy – may thus represent the vestigial memory of an ancient physical type. The 'nature spirit' explanation fails to answer the question of why certain physical elvish characteristics should persist in this way. Presumably, purely spiritual creatures wouldn't need ears at all – not even to listen to the bagpipes.
Doreen Greenwood, Stockport, Greater Manchester, 2004

FLYING BARBIE

As we drove home after visiting my in-laws in Hannastown, Greensburg, Pennsylvania, one day in the summer of 1998, something flew in front of our van. It was dark, after 9pm, and I was using the high beams so I could see any deer if they tried to cross the road. A few bugs could be seen heading toward the headlights of our mini van, then my wife and I saw what appeared to be a Barbie doll with insect wings. We had a good look at it for two to three seconds before it disappeared in front of the van. We were travelling about 50 mph (80km/h) so there was not much we could do but wait for the thud of it hitting the grill – but the sound never came. I pulled over and checked the grill, but found nothing.
I looked at my wife and joked, "I think we just ran over Tinkerbell".

I have seen many a locust in my time and I don't believe this was one; neither do I think it was a grasshopper. It had florescent wings that were oddly coloured. It was maybe just smaller than a Barbie. I have two girls so I know what a Barbie looks like.
Martin Garcia, by email, 2000

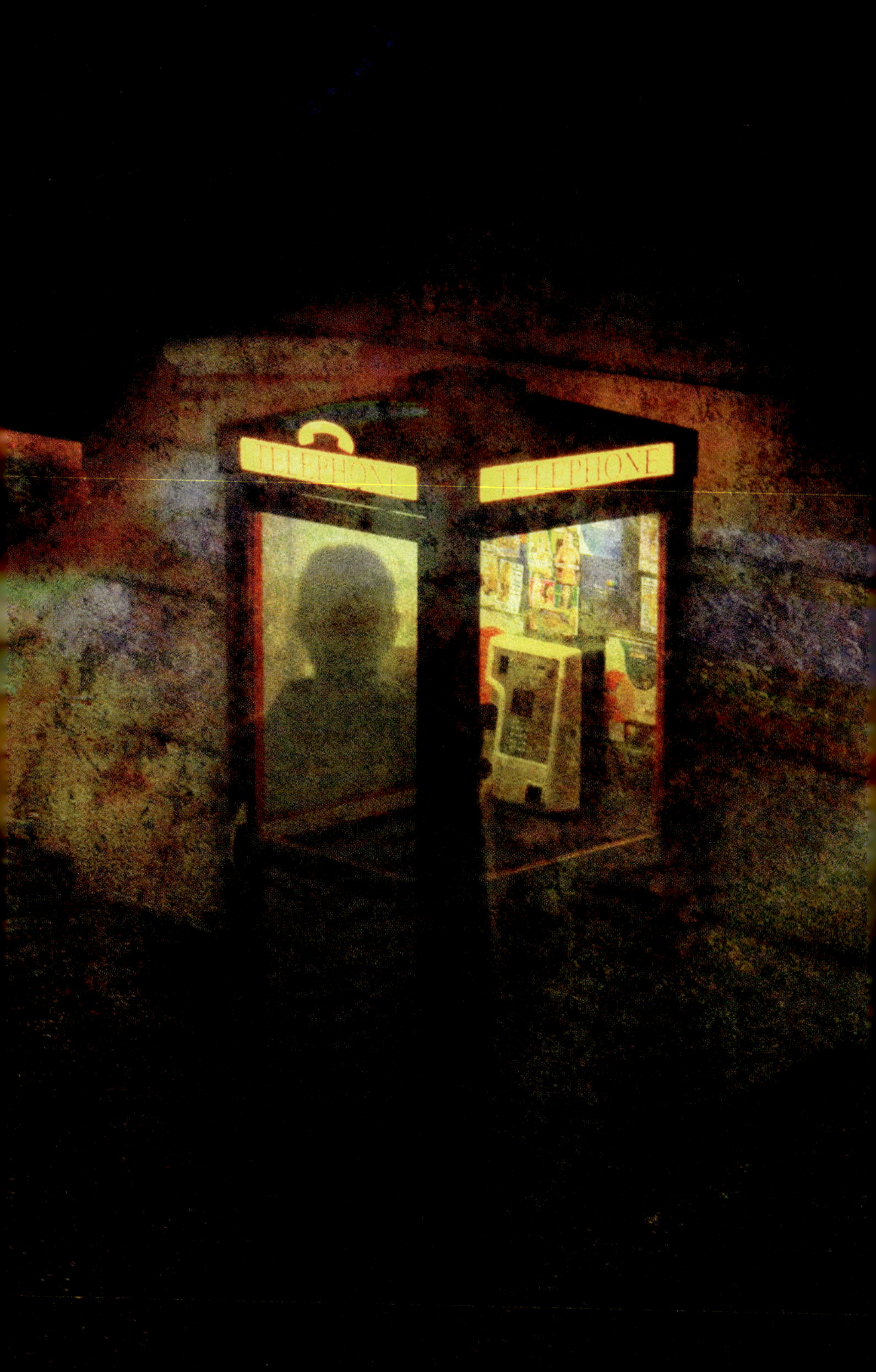
TELEPHONE
TELEPHONE

9 Down the Line

> For the layman, technological advances can be indistinguishable from magic – and indeed the telephone network sometimes appears to have a life of its own, connecting us to those whom we need to speak to or playing strange tricks on us. What's more, we can see no reason why poltergeists and the whole fiendish crew of a parallel universe can't make use of our mundane technology...

FREAKY PHONE CALLS

NO WIFE, NO FIRE

One day in the year 2000, I was alone in my New York apartment with my cat Polly when the telephone rang. An unfamiliar voice told me that "my wife" had just called to report that there was a "fire in my oven". I told the "doorman" that I had no wife and there was no fire in my oven. (Spookily, however, there *had* been a fire in my electric oven a week previously.)

Shortly after he hung up, there was a knock at my door. It was two white men in their thirties. They were in plain clothes and didn't offer any identification. They said they were from building security, even though I knew that all building security guards wear uniform. One of the men was very calm as he told me that "my wife" had called in to report a fire in my oven. I explained once again that I had no wife and no fire in my oven. The other man seemed to be in a violent rage and told the calm man that he was "going in", no matter what. His rage was very frightening.

Suddenly, Polly jumped up on a chair in plain view of the doorway. As soon as the calm one saw the cat, he grabbed the angry one by the shoulder and pulled him away. There was no question that seeing my cat had some sort of effect on the calm one. A few moments later, an authentic building security guard, with uniform and badge, appeared at my door, once again saying that "my wife" had called to report "the fire" in my oven. I denied both wife and fire, he shrugged his shoulders and left.

Who were these two men, one so relaxed, the other so furious? What was it about seeing the cat that caused them to retreat so suddenly? Who was the woman pretending to be my wife?
Ronald Rosenblatt, New York, 2002

PARALLEL UNIVERSE

I live in a converted warehouse in east London with a video entryphone by the front door. The camera has a fixed point of view and shows visitors against a background of the adjacent Victorian warehouse. The tiny TV entryphone unit in my flat hadn't shown a picture for a while, although the buzzer and intercom were working normally. The system was serviced – at the camera end rather than at my end – and to my amazement when the doorbell rang I could clearly see my visitor on the screen as intended, but against the background of a row of Edwardian terraced houses that I'd never seen before.

Is someone in that unidentified street seeing our warehouses on their video entry phone? Has a time-space portal been unwittingly opened? Is this a ghost in the machine that throws into doubt the veracity of modern surveillance equipment? I subsequently learnt that a neighbour has had this illogical view on his entryphone for months. The repair company suggests that he has a second-hand monitor with its last view burned into the screen; he says he bought it as a new unit; and of course this doesn't explain why my monitor has only recently taken to depicting my visitors in a parallel universe (though some of them definitely are). If anyone has unwanted warehouses on their video entryphone maybe they would consider an exchange.
Alex Brattell, by email, 1995

IT'S NOT FOR YOU-HOO

I work for a government body in electronic engineering, specifically concerning equipment like fax machines. In 1989 I was paged over the building public address to go to my office as there was a call waiting. The conversation went as follows:

"Mr Haines?"

"Yes."

DOWN THE LINE IT HAPPENED TO ME!

> "*Who were these uniformed men? Who was the woman pretending to be my wife?*"

"It's about the order for teleprinter paper you placed at the exhibition."
"No I didn't. I wasn't there."
"That is Mr D.A. Haines, spelt H.A.I.N.E.S.?"
"Yes."
"Well, it's your name on the order."
"It can't be. I don't deal with teleprinters, only fax machines."
"Your telephone number is 708 2399 extension 35?"
"Yes, that's my number alright."
"And you are Mr Dave Haines?"
"No, it's Dale, actually."
"Well, it looks like Dave. Anyway that's what it says here, 10 boxes of paper for British Telecom Stores."
"I don't work for BT, I work for —— ——."
"Oh! It says BT in the order, Birmingham depot."
"Where?"
"Birmingham."
"What number did you dial?"
"021 708 2399 extension 35."
"You've got 01 708 2399 extension 35. This is south London, not Birmingham. You dropped the 2 from the number."
"Oh, sorry. Goodbye."
Click, buzz, whirr.
DA Haines, Bromley, Kent, 1992

CROSSED LINES

After my husband, Major General Sir Roy Redgrave, retired, I worked in London as a freelance negotiator with an estate agent in Chelsea. One of my colleagues, Claire Townley, was to marry an Italian/American banker, Jay Runneowitsch, whom she had met in the course of her work.

One afternoon during the spring of 1985, some time after Claire had left the company, the telephone on my desk rang, and I answered it with the usual "Carlyle and Co. May I help you?" The voice then replied, "Sorry, we seem to have a crossed line. I thought I was receiving an incoming call, but since you are Carlyle and Co, may I speak to Lady Redgrave?" It was Jay Runneowitsch. He then explained to me that the telephone had, in fact, rung on his desk, that he had not made an outgoing call and had picked it up only to hear my voice.

While he and I were chatting and remarking on how unusual it must be to get a crossed line with someone one knew and what a coincidence it was, I noticed a Range Rover pulling up outside the office. "Hang on a moment," I said to Jay, as in walked none other than Claire, whom I had not seen for several months. She was absolutely stunned to be told that her husband-to-be was on the line. What had happened, Claire Townley explained, was that driving along the Fulham Road she had had a sudden urge to visit her former office and decided then and there to drop in, on the spur of the moment.

Valerie Redgrave, London, 2001

A few years ago, I answered the telephone to a shy voice saying, "It's Sue here. Could I speak to Chris?" I was pleased, because my brother Chris had mentioned recently meeting a delightful girl called Sue. I called him to the phone. A merry conversation ensued, during the course of which it dawned on them both that this Sue was a stranger who had rung the wrong number trying to contact a different Chris. However, they got on so well that one thing led to another, and now they are married. That other Sue and Chris are gratefully remembered for the catalytic part they played in this story.

Mrs M Carroll, Stopham, West Sussex, 2001

PHONE HOME

Earlier this year I paid a visit to Amsterdam with a friend. My mobile phone wouldn't work over there, but my friend's phone did, albeit infrequently. Late on the night that we arrived there, my friend's phone rang but stopped ringing before he could answer it. Checking the unanswered calls facility revealed that the number that had just rung was that of my flat. I live on my own and the only people apart from me who have keys for the flat would have had no way of knowing my friend's number. Amsterdam is an environment rather conducive to paranoia at the best of times but I'd bet I was by far the most paranoid person there that night.

Alun Cureton, Telford, Shropshire, 2001

DISTRESS CALLS

HOME ALONE

In 1991 I was 19 and studying at art college in Ireland. With the help of my college I obtained a temporary work visa for the US and travelled to California to look for work. I lived with a college mate who had made the journey with me and I enjoyed nothing more than the rare times that I had the house to myself. One evening at around seven o'clock I was in the house alone when the phone rang. The caller appeared to be a little girl in distress. She told me that her mummy was gone and that she was at home alone. There was something about what she said that made me suspicious (I think it was something about my location but I can't remember what exactly). Though it really sounded like a child, I thought that it could also be a woman doing an excellent impression of a child. Not wanting to take the chance that it wasn't a child left alone, I instructed her not to leave the house and that if her mummy didn't return by the time it got dark, then she was to telephone the police and tell them where she was. After making sure that she understood my instructions but still a little suspicious, I said goodbye and hung up. It was a strange experience – if it wasn't a child, why would someone do that? And if it was a scam, what was the payoff?

I thought nothing more of the incident until back in Ireland about a year and a half later I was walking along with my best friend who had travelled to Canada the summer after I had been in the States. I told him about my weird phone call, which prompted him to tell me about a weird phone call he had received whilst living in Vancouver during the summer of 1992. Alone in the house he was living in, he took a call from a little girl whose mummy had left her in the house alone. He thought there was something suspicious about her due to something she said (he couldn't remember either). He thought that she could be an adult doing an impression of a child, but gave her pretty much the same advice that I had given a year previously and hung up.

If this is an example of some sort of Munchausen's syndrome or telephone scam then my friend and I are the only people I know who have experienced it, a year apart and in separate countries. People have suggested that it was a wind-up by a friend. I'm sure with a little effort, friends back home could have obtained our numbers in the States and Canada – but if it was a joke it wasn't particularly funny and no one has come forward to claim responsibility. Perhaps it was part of some larger scale fraud or medical condition that I am unaware of.

Francis Lowe, Nottingham, 2004

THE LITTLE VOICE

In 1996 I was living in Highgate, London, and spending long periods alone immersed in writing. Late one weekday afternoon I received a phone call from a little girl who said she was alone and didn't know where her mummy was. Like Francis Lowe, I listened closely for signs that an adult was making the call as I talked to her for at least five minutes, but I never really thought that she could have been more than five years old. By the end of the conversation I think the girl had become quite calm. At no time was she ever in great distress; she was scared but not hysterical. I asked her name but cannot recall her answer; I also asked where she lived, to which she gave a 'don't know'-type response. It was as if the conversation could not move forward beyond the premise of 'I'm alone, I'm scared'. I did ask her if she wanted me to call the police, but again this led nowhere.

After our conversation, I vaguely recall dialling 1471 and getting no number, at least not one I noted. This could all be put down to imagination had it not been that very soon after the incident – no more than a day or two – I wrote a story called "Dread Country" in which a protagonist very much like myself is repeatedly called by an old woman in distress. Something about the process of writing this eerie story expunged any need I had to think about the incident that

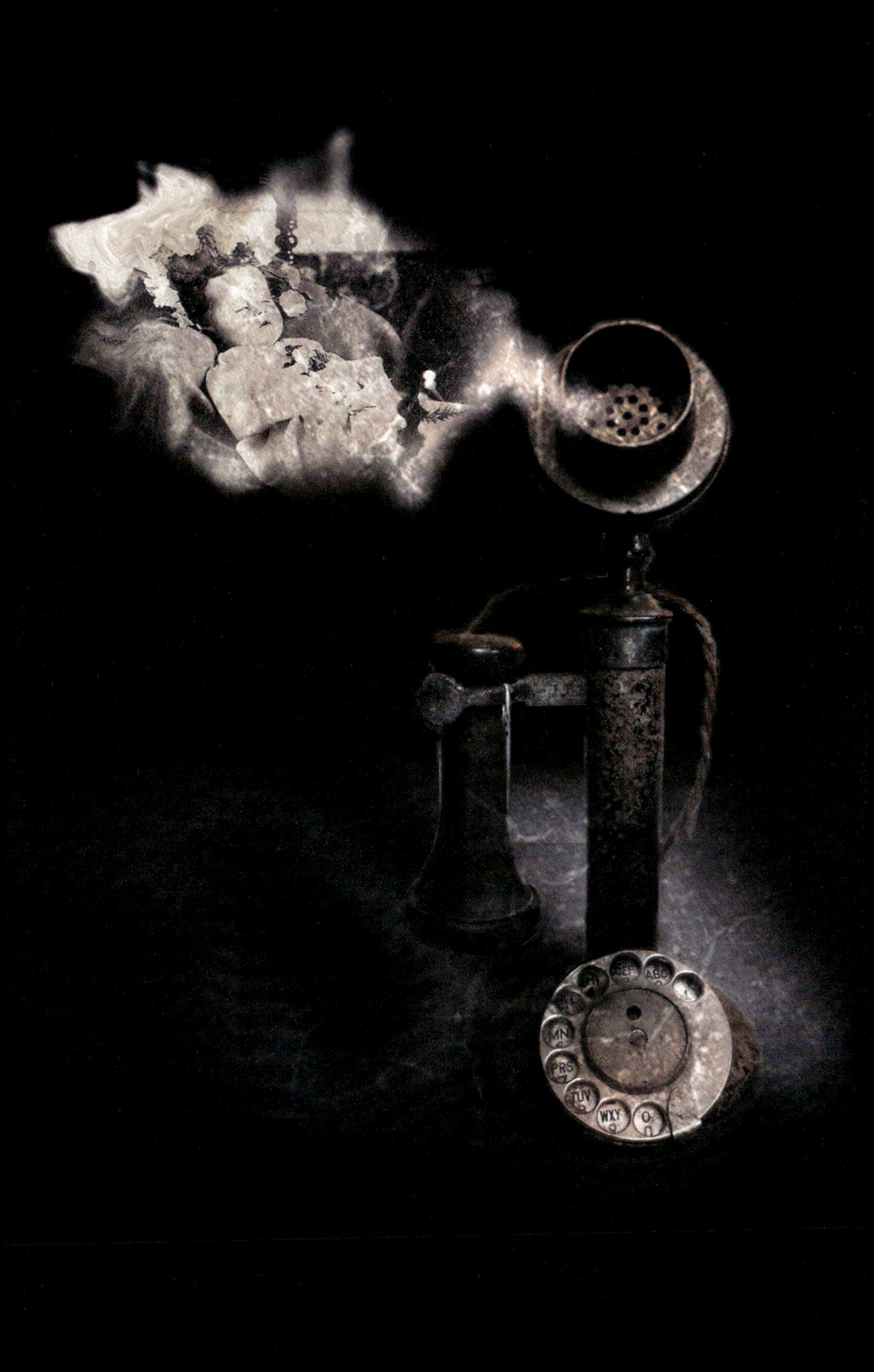
PRS
TUV
WXY

had inspired it and I never gave it much thought again until now. My attitude at the time was that it had even chances of being a prank, one of those weird metropolitan-life things that happens, yet with every similar tale that emerges I am less certain of choosing to explain the incident as a prank (either played by the caller or my own mind) rather than a genuine cry for help or a more paranormal event.

If pressed, I would look towards a theory that defines a kind of psychological 'phase-shift', something on the lines of a waking-dream that is created by psychic stress. This kind of event is quite distinct from hypnagogia, dreaming, or sleepwalking, since the subject always remains fully alert and conscious. At such times the mind 'intersects' with reality, creating an event that is, to all 'objective' understanding, both real and unreal. The key is that the receiver of the call is always alone (at least in all the reports I've seen). Having experienced vivid states of altered awareness in my childhood, all of them involving a strong auditory aspect, I cannot discount the possibility that I may still be susceptible to these 'interjections'. How can we ever know all our own minds? Unless a few of these strange calls are recorded or the callers are backtraced, we will never know what or who produces the Little Voice, and maybe not even then.
Jerry Glover, by email, 2005

HELP ME, SUSIE'S DYING

Back around 1975 when I was nine, some of the kids I knocked around with insisted we all pile into the nearest phone box to hear a spooky message. By dialling a number – I think made up of zeros, ones and twos – and without needing to insert two pence, a woman, speaking in a curiously monotone voice, could be heard saying "Help me, help me, Susie's dying", over and over. Some of the lads said she sometimes said "Help me, help me, Susie's drowning". Was it some weird engineer's test signal (hence no money needed)?
Rob Dickinson, Worsthorne, Lancashire, 2000

I can remember once cramming into a phone box in the Stoneyholme area of Burnley with various other kids to hear the strange message related by Rob Dickinson. I cannot remember the number dialled. Could this be an early example of EVP (Electronic Voice Phenomenon), or just explicable interference on the telephone system, filtered through the active imaginations of young witnesses?
Christopher McDermott, London, 2000

" A voice could be heard saying 'Help me, help me, Susie's dying', over and over "

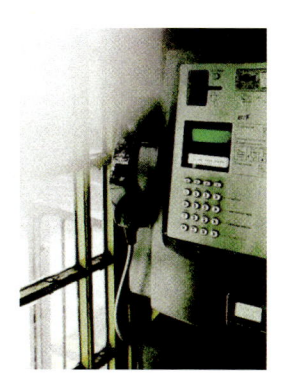

I remember the spooky message when I was a child playing with the old red phone boxes in Burnley. Two phone boxes in particular were prone to mysterious scary voice messages – one at the top of Dalton Street on Planetree Estate and the other at the end of Harold Street on Stoops Estate. As I remember, you put 2p in the slot and pressed 20 20 20 20 and the voice on the other end would be crackly but audible: "Help me, Susie's dying", which would send us kids running in all directions.
AG Russell-Dallamore, by email, 2003

I am from Burnley and have a vivid memory of the said phone message. In either 1980 or 1981, three other girls and myself were loitering with the intent not to go back to school after lunch. We were messing around in a phone box near to school, calling random numbers and talking rubbish if anyone answered (well, we thought it was funny!).

One of the girls said she knew a number you could call to hear a "spooky message" – I think there were 3s and 2s in it. When she called this number we all heard the message as quoted in previous correspondence. I have no doubts as to the phrasing of what I heard. It was a clear voice with no audible distortion. Needless to say, we were all a bit freaked out by this and when a British Telecom van pulled up nearby we made a hasty retreat and returned to school.
Tracey Maclean, Knaresbourough, North Yorkshire, 2003

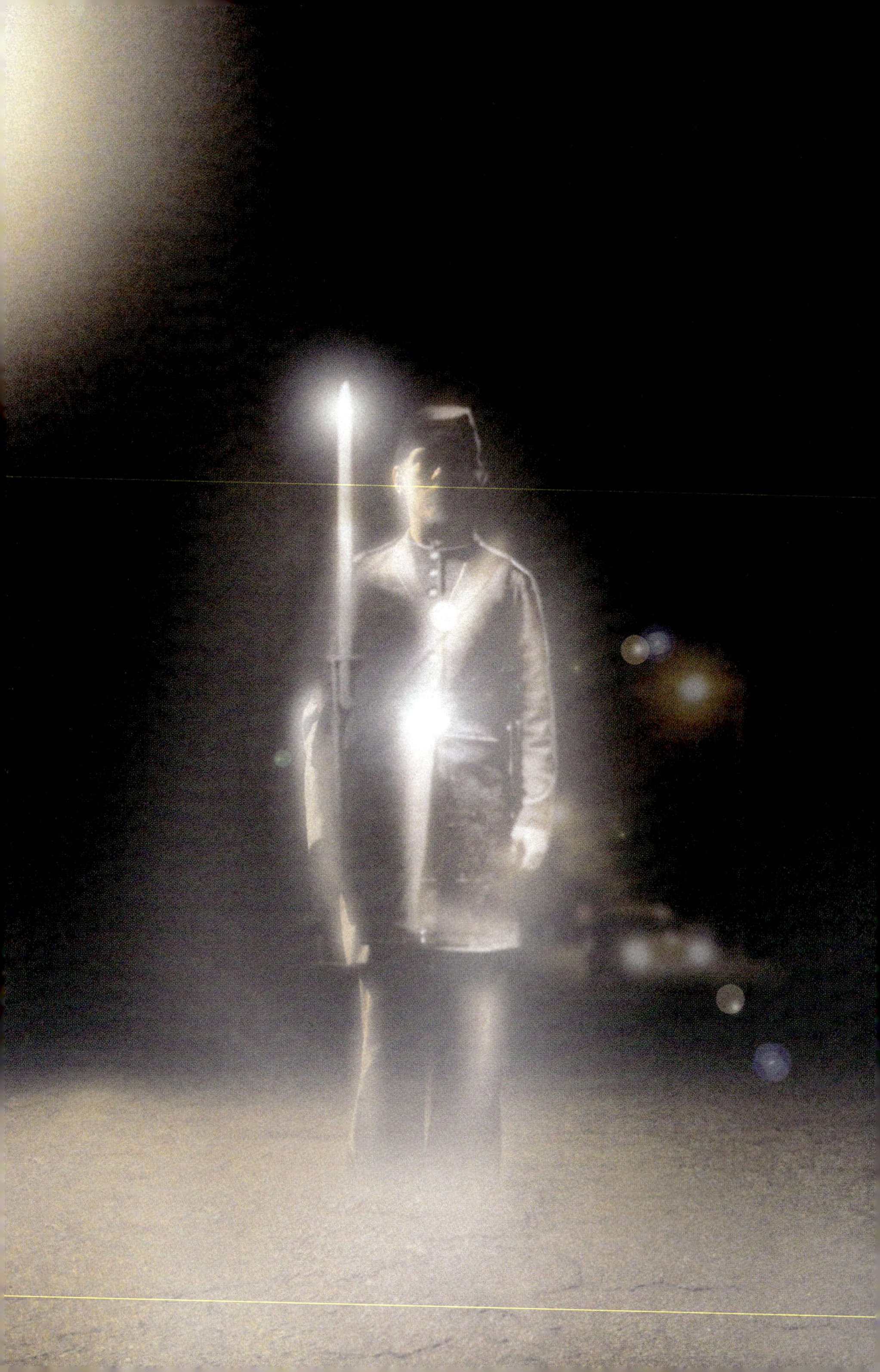

10 On the Road

Roads – those liminal spaces between one place and another – are the location for all sorts of strange encounters, especially late at night when they can take on an eerie sense of strangeness. Spooky travellers' tales abound: the driver who sees a monster silhouetted in his headlights, a goblin reflected in his wing mirror, or a phantom materialising in the path of his speeding car…

HAUNTED HIGHWAYS

GETTYSBURG STRAGGLER
The only ghost sighting of my life took place in the middle of a road, around midnight in the dead of winter. I was around 10 years old, which would make this the mid-1970s. I lived with my family in a small town in central Virginia. We would often drive to Pennsylvania, especially around the holidays, to spend time with our relatives there.

This particular trip found us driving late at night down a lonely stretch of Highway 81 about 30 miles (48km) north-west of Gettysburg, Pennsylvania. My father was clutching the steering wheel and staring intently at the patch of light thrown out by the headlights.

The next few moments were what he recalled recently as "still the strangest thing that ever happened to me". I remember seeing a figure in the gloom up ahead, a man walking, an odd thing to be doing on a major highway on a very cold night miles from anywhere. As we came closer we realised to our horror that he was walking down the middle of the lane we were on and we were going to hit him. No one screamed – there wasn't enough time.

That moment before we were going to flatten him seemed to stretch out for minutes. I could tell it was a man by the width of the shoulders and his gait. He was wearing a very long grey coat that came to about his knees. He had pants of the same colour, which were tucked into beat-up, dirty leather boots; in fact he seemed kind of dirty and ragged all over. On his back was a backpack with a bedroll attached. He wore a small cap, also grey, of the type I've only seen in pictures of Civil War soldiers. In his left hand he carried some very long object that from behind looked exactly like a rifle butt. The really bizarre thing was that although he was walking very purposefully and erect, not staggering or weaving, he seemed to be completely and utterly oblivious to the fact that we were closing on him at around 60mph (96km/h).

There was no time to hit the brakes. My dad jerked the wheel to the left and the car lurched toward the passing lane. It was too late, we were going too fast and he was too close to us. We expected a sickening dull thud, but it never came. My dad got control of the car and slowed down. If we had missed him, it was by a matter of inches. As we swerved, I looked out the side and then rear windows of the car expecting to see him in the glow of the taillights, but I could see nothing but road.

The fact that he was dressed exactly like a Civil War Confederate soldier and that we were near Gettysburg, the site of the bloodiest and most decisive battle of the Civil War, was forgotten for the moment. We decided that he was a drunk and/or insane drifter bent on suicide. At that time we didn't even consider that this might not be an actual flesh-and-blood person. He was too solid-looking for us to think that he might be an apparition.

Several miles down the road we stopped at the entrance to the Pennsylvania Turnpike for the last leg of our journey. My father talked to the man in the tollbooth and told him about the crazy man wandering down the middle of the highway. The toll taker very unexpectedly laughed and said something like, "Ah! I guess the ghosts are out wandering again tonight!" My dad got mad at his levity and we didn't leave till he got an assurance that there would be a Highway Patrol car sent out to investigate. The toll-taker probably never did send out a patrol car because he knew what we didn't until much later, that around Gettysburg people seeing wandering Civil War soldiers isn't really that unusual.
Michael Mcquate, San Francisco, 2002

PHANTOM STAGECOACH LEAVES TRACKS
In 1968, I was working as the driver for the mail clerk of the US Army's 560th Signal Battalion stationed at Caserma Ederle in Vicenza, Italy. My duties included

> *I saw the black silhouette of a stagecoach crossing the road from left to right...*

driving the clerk and his assistant to several outlying radio relay sites to deliver the mail.

A sudden snowstorm had dumped two or three inches of heavy, wet snow on the ground by the time we left Caserma Ederle at half past ten on the morning of 24 January. As we entered the countryside on the outskirts of Vicenza we were travelling on a two-lane road atop a 12-ft-(3.7m) high dyke running straight down the middle of a large, open field. The blanket of white covering the road and field was broken only by a small, single storey building to the left of the road a few hundred yards from the edge of town. Ours was the first vehicle to travel this road since the snow had begun falling. There were absolutely no tracks of any kind on or near the road.

Suddenly, about 70 yards (64m) ahead, I saw the black silhouette of a stagecoach crossing the road from right to left. Perched in the driver's seat was a man wearing a top hat. He too was in silhouette. His arms were extended out in front of his body as though he were holding a pair of reins. Neither reins nor horses, however, were a part of the silhouette, which disappeared at the left shoulder of the road.

"Did you see that?" I yelled to my passengers. Engaged in conversation, they had not. I explained what I had seen and stopped the jeep as we neared the spot where the silhouette had crossed the road. There, in the freshly fallen snow, were two parallel tracks approximately 4ft (1m) apart, each being about 2in (5cm) in width! The tracks began at the crest of the dyke on the right, crossed the road, descended the embankment and ran another 20 yards (18m) before disappearing into a jumble of bicycles parked against the building mentioned above. There were no footprints or other tracks in the area. Neither was there a nearby door through which two particularly agile cyclists might have escaped. The nearest door, in fact, was around a corner some 60ft (18m) away and there were no prints leading in or out of it.

Later that year while visiting Borlum Farm overlooking Loch Ness, I met the owner's father, John Gordon-Dean, a retired RAF officer. His unsolicited account of a similar experience went as follows. He was driving through the Midlands just prior to World War II when a stagecoach, complete with horses and driver and in full, living colour, simply materialized in his pathway. He took to the ditch causing considerable damage to his Bugatti and slight injury to himself. Certain of what he had seen and unwilling to accept hallucination as the cause, he scoured local records until he was able to establish that the spot where he had seen the coach was located along one of the major north-south stage routes of the 19th century. The coach itself left no physical evidence.
Mike Owens, Pekin. Illinois, 1989

HIGHWAY APPARITION

In October 1971, when I was 26, single, and living in Oulton Broad, Lowestoft, I spent an evening in Yarmouth with friends. We had a few beers, but as I was driving, I kept my intake low. I set off alone for home in my Opel Rekord car. It was a clear night, and I just about had the road to myself. I may well have been going over the speed limit; after all, the road was clear and there wasn't a soul in sight.

At about 12.30am on the Gorleston Road near the old Oulton Primary School, an elderly woman suddenly appeared in front of the car. She half turned towards me, but because of her hood, I couldn't see her features clearly. I slammed on the brakes, knowing there was no way I could miss her. Horrified, I got out of the car, convinced there would be a mangled body – but when I reached the spot there was no body, no blood, nothing. Nor did the car show any signs of impact. I went back further along the road in case I had misjudged the place, but found nothing. By the following morning, I was certain I'd seen a ghost. In the local library I found a story of a hooded woman being seen in Gorleston Road. It was suggested she had been killed on her way home after visiting someone in Lowestoft.
Clive Thrower, by email, 2002

PERSON-SHAPED HOLE

I was a student at Birmingham University at the beginning of the 1980s, but used to drive home to Nottingham most Friday nights, returning to Birmingham on the following Sunday. The journey was about 50 miles (80km) each way, and it was on one such drive home that I witnessed a phenomenon for which I have absolutely no explanation.

Part of my journey used to take me along a straight country road through the village of Lount in Derbyshire. Just before the village, there is a steep hill (downhill in the direction I was going) as it passes Lount landfill site. It was dark, though the moon was out. There were no streetlights on that stretch of road, but my car headlights were lit. As I passed the entrance to the landfill site, I was suddenly aware of a figure running into the path of my car from the opposite side of the road. The figure wasn't so much a shadow as a silhouette. The edges were clearly defined, but there were no details to be seen. It was just as if someone had cut a person-shaped hole in space itself.

From the size and shape, I estimate that it was a boy of maybe 13 years old. The shape ran in front of my car before I had a chance to take evasive action. In that instant, I hit the brakes and braced for the impact. The car slewed to a halt, but there was no bump. I pulled the car into a lay-by a little way down the road, and made a good search, but there was nobody to be seen. No bump, no body and no signs of anything untoward. I sat in the car, upset and shaking for a good five minutes, and then continued on my way.

Chris Shilling, by email, 2003

TERRIFYING TRAVELLERS

TENNESSEE DOG-MAN

I live in the eastern mountain region of Tennessee and work second shift at a factory in Dayton, a town about 25 miles (40km) away, with a mountain in between. I usually don't start for home until at least 12.30am. We don't all get out at the same time, so sometimes I'm the only one on the highway.

One night during the winter of 2003/2004 I was coming across the mountain. There are quite a few houses along the way, and a lot of them have outside lights on all night long, so it's not pitch black. Anyway, I was coming down a straight

stretch of highway when I saw a man on the side of the road on my right walking toward me. He was wearing a light-coloured shirt with dark pants. As I got closer to him, he suddenly turned his back toward me and bent over. I slowed down quite a bit and went toward the centre of the highway as I was about to pass him. When I got close to him, I saw that this person was now a huge dog and he peered around to look at me as I passed. This 'thing' had a long snout and large teeth like a dog or wolf and was sort of grinning at me. I passed it and tried to look at it in my rear view mirror, but couldn't see anything. I was flabbergasted and I've gone over and over it in my mind ever since trying to figure out what I actually saw.
Patricia Law, Pikeville, Tennessee, 2005

A SHAGGY SHAPE
About two years ago, my husband and I visited friends in York. We left them at approximately 12.45am and I drove home while my husband slept in the passenger seat. The last stretch of road before home is about 1-2 miles (1.6-3.2km) long with two roundabouts roughly 1 mile (1.6km) apart. The road between these roundabouts is a gentle hill with wide grass verges and low banks lined with trees.

About halfway to the bridge, the hairs stood up on the back of my neck and I was overcome with terror. Having crossed the bridge, I saw, standing on the kerb to my left, a 7ft (2.1m)-tall "shaggy shape" about 4ft (1.2m) wide and covered from head to foot in long dark hair; it had no visible face or limbs. In the split second that I saw it, I turned away, as I got the feeling that if I looked directly at this 'thing' I would die. I accelerated past it and glancing in my rear-view mirror I saw it shuffle off the kerb and into the road where I had just been.
Mrs DJ Singleton, Farsley, Leeds, 1997

DARK PASSERS-BY
One day some 20-odd years ago, when I was about 10 or 11 years old, I was bicycling in Sheffield along Ecclesfield Road, known locally as "The Woodbottom".

It winds along for about a mile and a half (2.4km) between Wincobank and Shiregreen, with no turnoffs. On one side of the road is a wooded hillside (Wooley Woods) and on the other a line of trees behind which is a railway line and, further back, some industrial units. It was Saturday afternoon, around 4:30pm, when the incident occurred. I can confirm this as when I got home the football

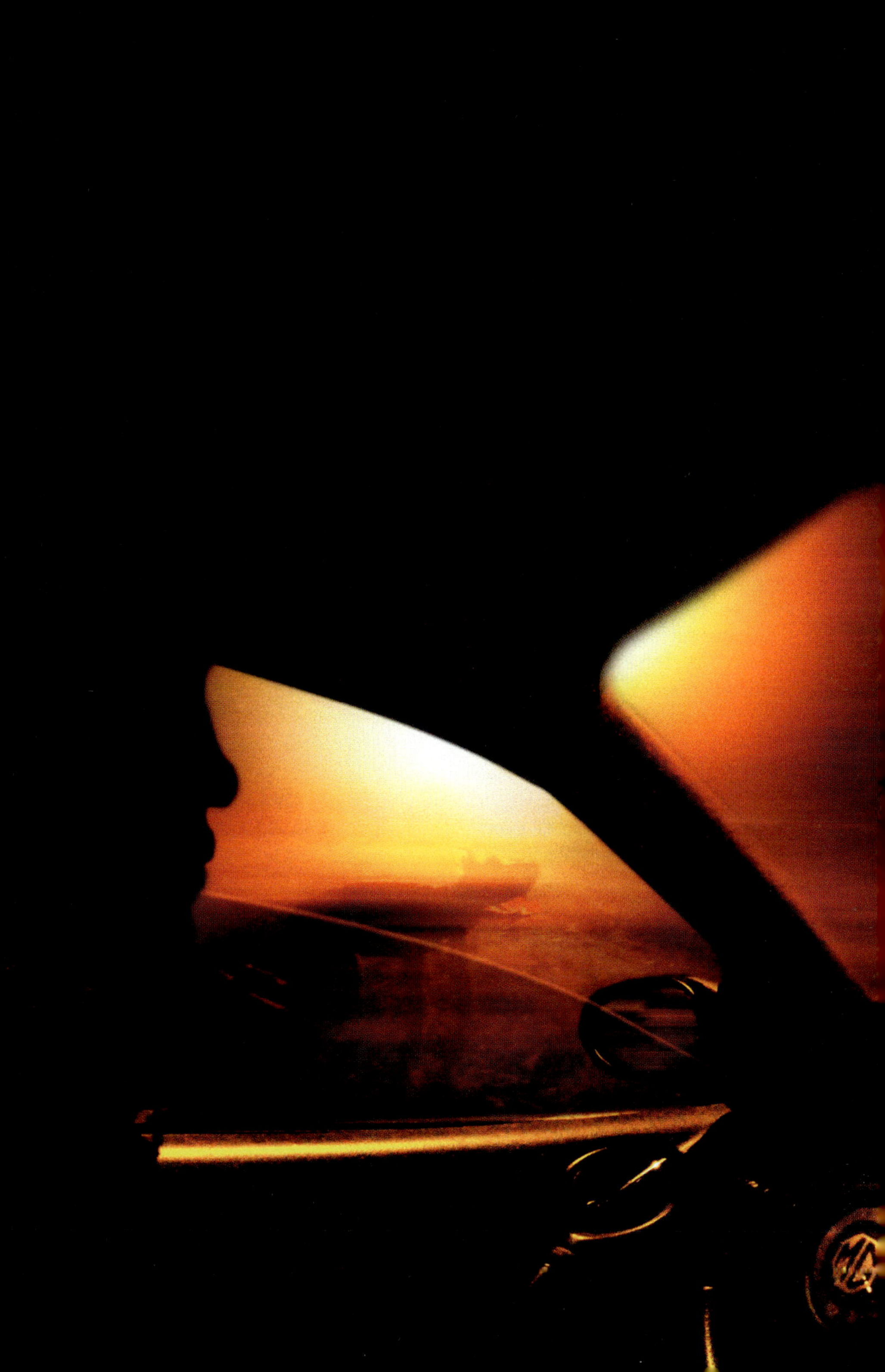

results were on the telly.

I was cycling back from Shiregreen towards Wincobank where I lived. The Woodbottom was empty of traffic, which in retrospect seems odd for that time on a Saturday. As I peddled along, something made me look round. As I did, a car came around the bend behind me.

The car drew up alongside and kept pace with me. It was black, with all the windows blacked out or heavily tinted. I had no interest in cars and could not identify a make or model. It looked a little like a taxi-cab without the taxi light. However, the strangest thing about the vehicle was what sounded like a cacophony of shouting voices coming from inside it.

As the car kept pace and began to get nearer to me, I began to panic. My front wheel jammed against the kerb and as I tried to turn the handlebars I was catapulted over them, landing on a grass verge, dazed and frightened. I lifted my head to see the car shoot off towards Wincobank.

Some moments later, as I lay on the grass, I heard the sound of an engine, and saw a man on a moped coming along the road from Wincobank. He looked straight at me, turned in the road and pulled up alongside. Without saying a word, he checked me for broken bones, stood my bike up and put the chain back on.

Eventually he asked me what had happened. I mumbled something but it probably wasn't coherent. He was in his mid-forties, with greying hair and a grey beard. When I had finished my rambling explanation he nodded his head but made no comment. He asked me if I would be alright and I assured him I would as I was almost home anyway. Then – and this is what disturbs me the most – the man rode off towards Wincobank, *the direction he had come from.*

I cannot shake my conviction that the man on the moped expected to find me there. Not only that, but I believe his sole purpose was to see that I was okay. What is difficult to convey in words is how bloody strange the whole scenario felt, right from the moment I first saw the car.

Darren R Scothern, Sheffield, 1998

WARRINGTON'S WEIRD ROUNDABOUT

I think this odd event happened in 1990 or 1991; I can't give a precise date. Three of us who lived in the Warrington area had been to see a midnight movie at the UCI complex. I was driving and had agreed to give the other two a lift back to Latchford and Grappenhall. It was around 2am and raining heavily. We passed

" *The car was black, with all the windows blacked out or heavily tinted...* "

through Warrington centre and headed to Latchford. The area is only a few minutes from the centre of Warrington and is still urban – in no way remote.

We approached a roundabout and I noticed something unusual – a white Toyota saloon was parked up right in the middle of the roundabout, actually on the grass centre. I thought it had been stolen and abandoned, as it had no obvious accident damage. We then noticed that there were two strange-looking occupants. This will sound stupid, but both of them had huge heads, one which looked like a giant upright raisin, no obvious features, and one whose head in profile was shaped like the African continent, with a protruding dome to the back of the head. Both seemed to have dark glasses on and were looking directly ahead. Both heads seemed to be very dark and leathery in texture.

As it was late, dark and raining heavily, we were unsure about what we had seen, so I circled the roundabout twice more to get a better look. Yep, they did have two massive, misshapen heads and seemed to be wearing dark glasses.

They didn't look like they were in trouble, and as it was lashing down and I had to drive back to Widnes after dropping the other two blokes off, we just looked at each other, said wtf? and carried on.
James xxx, by email, 2002

CUT-OUT MAN
Some years ago, after a night of general chat, a friend and I were walking from another friend's house to my own in the leafy suburb of Brockley in south-east London. I had drunk only tea or soft drinks all night and had consumed no drugs whatsoever. It was around 6am and dawn was breaking when we saw a figure

walking up the street towards us. The word we coined later to describe its movement was 'lolloping' – a kind of up and down bouncy walk. It took a few seconds for the two of us to realise this was no human being. "See that man?" I asked. "Yes." "It's not a man, though, is it?" I found myself saying. "No,' said my friend, sounding scared. "It isn't."

The creature was entirely black and like a cardboard cutout, flat and one-dimensional. It had no features at all, and arms that hung down to its knees. It seemed to be ignoring us, then seemed to realise we could see it and began to 'lollop' faster towards us. We ran to my front door and hid in the hallway as quiet and unmoving as possible when we saw the thing – we felt it was male – approach the front door and appear to look through the glass from the way its head moved up and down and around. It then turned away.

We didn't sleep for some time after that, discussing what we saw. It was shaped like many descriptions of 'greys', but both of us came away with the impression that what we saw was not of this world but from a parallel dimension. We instinctively felt it was not a creature to try and communicate with, and not something that it was good to be near. We felt that if this creature had somehow got hold of us, we would not be around today to tell the tale.

Andy Hinkinson-Hodnett, by email, 2005

MIDSUMMER MONSTER

There was nothing much for teenagers to do in Ballynahinch, our small village in County Down, so we used to pile into each other's cars and go driving in the evenings. Sometimes we played hide-and-seek: one car had a 10-minute head start to 'hide' and we timed how long it took the other car to find us. This was no mean task, as the network of little roads and lanes leading up to farmland is endless in this part of the world.

On Midsummer's Eve 1998, it had been our turn to hide. There were five of us in the car altogether and I was in the front passenger seat. We had found a brilliant hiding place by reversing up a long, winding track, wide enough for only one vehicle. With the lights turned off we were undetectable from the road. Once our eyes became accustomed, we could easily see our surroundings in the moonlight. After about two minutes listening to the dulcet tones of The Cure, an almost overwhelming feeling of 'eeriness' seemed to take over everyone at once, accompanied by a thumping sound and vibrations of heavy footfalls coming from behind us. The driver needed little persuading to get out of there fast.

ON THE ROAD   IT HAPPENED TO ME!

As soon as the car was moving, my friends in the back seat started yelling that they could see something following us in the field beyond the hedge on the passenger side, and I could feel its footfalls. We frantically rolled up all the open windows. It then overtook the passenger window and was level with the bonnet. It must have been running at 30mph (48km/h) at least to keep up with us.

I can only describe what I saw as a very tall humanoid. It ran (or rather loped) on muscular legs, which we could see through the sparse hedge. It had odd, elongated facial features from the side, almost like a buckrabbit with horns. Its chest, arms and torso were clearly visible as it was at least 3ft (90cm) taller than the hedge, which we later estimated was at least 5ft (1.5m) high. It was covered with what looked like very course, shaggy, sandy-coloured hair. I could see its nipples. As it ran level with the bonnet for about 30 seconds it turned its head as if to look directly in the car, and I got a full view of its face. It was goatlike, with two horns, a long face, and black, expressionless eyes on either side of its head. We were all mesmerised and couldn't look away; I don't know how my friend managed to keep driving.

The creature then headed away from the car, across the field, and out of sight. It was definitely on two legs, not four, and the muscular hindquarters ended in slim ankles with hooves. When we finally reached the end of the track, we encountered a ram with full horns standing in the middle of the road as we turned into it. Its eyes seemed to glow malevolently in the headlights. Thoroughly unnerved, we drove straight home.

There was definitely something 'otherworldly' about the creature we had seen. We still talk about it when we meet up. My friends, obviously swayed by the fact that it happened on Midsummer night, still maintain it was the god Pan or one of his variations, but I have other ideas. Could it have been an Irish 'pookie' or hobgoblin, or even old forky-tail himself – Lucifer? I later learned that at the time of the sighting there *was* a black magic circle operating in the area. Perhaps they were dabbling in invocations, unaware of what they were summoning up.

Amanda-Jayne Clayden, Ballynahinch, Co. Down, Northern Ireland, 2005

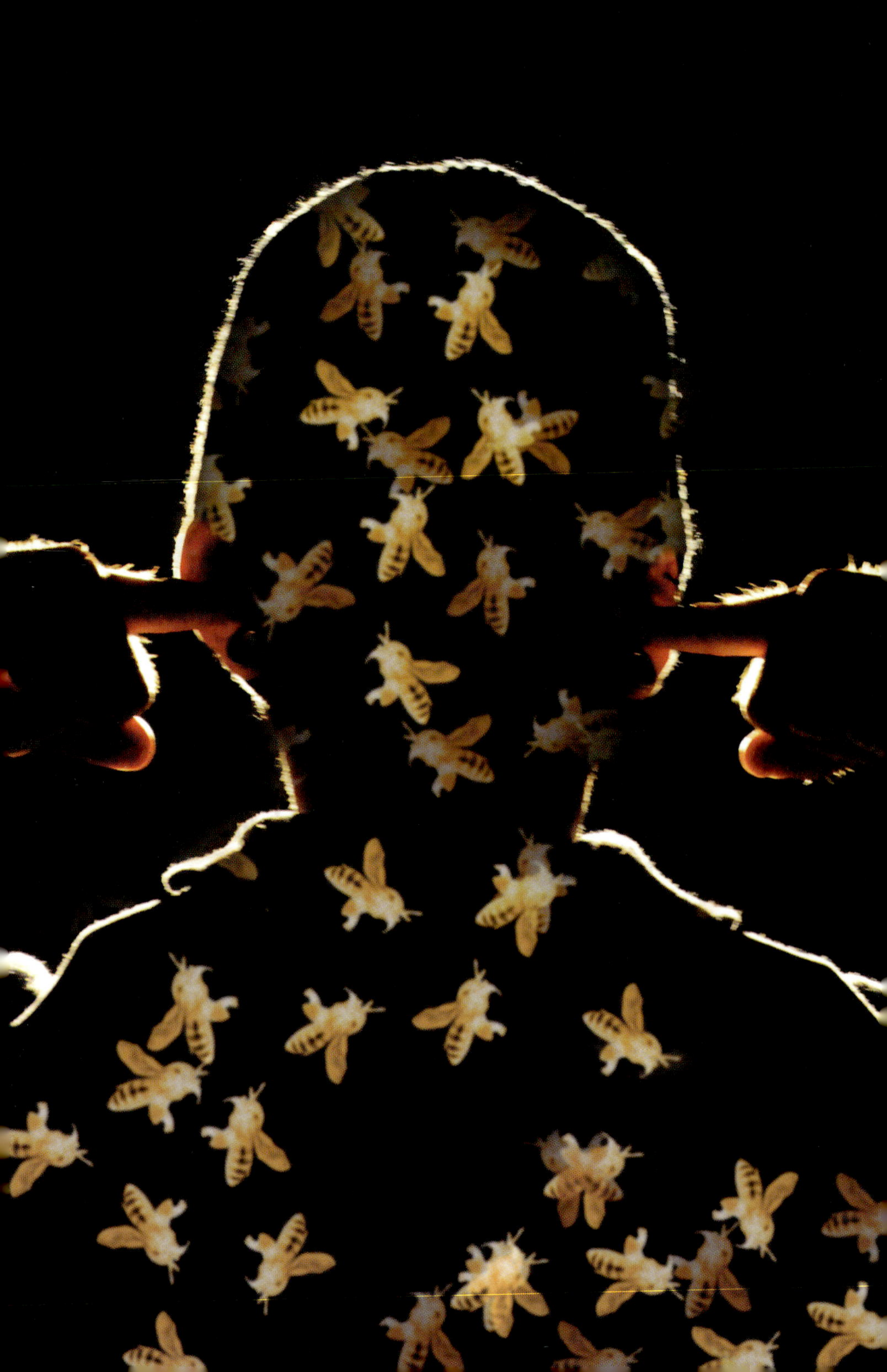

11 Hearing Things

> It can be a hum sounding like thousands of insects or the rumble of untraceable machinery, the distant laughter of invisible children, the uplifting strains of heavenly choirs, or the distant sounds of a battle fought centuries before. Some will say that these letter writers have just been "hearing things", but the explanation for many of these spooky sounds remains elusive...

THE HUMMADRUZ

BOTTLED NOISE
For the past couple of years I have been aware of an intermittently audible low frequency hum in the environment for which I can find no explanation. It occurs at irregular intervals and varies in duration between one and 10 seconds. I can best describe it as similar to the sound one gets when blowing into the neck of a bottle. I particularly notice the sound during the night, or at quiet times during the day. Living in a rural part of Ayrshire, I nevertheless associated the hum with some sort of industrial process. However, spending holidays in a remote part of the Hebrides, my husband and I occasionally hear the same sound. Having ruled out imaginary sounds, ear problems, foghorns and industrial processes, I am keen to find an explanation.
Mazda Munn, Dalry, Ayrshire, 1997

HI FI, LOW HUM
Further to Mazda Munn's letter, I am reminded of the attention paid to the unexplainable hums and buzzes back in the late 1970s. Much of it could be – and was – explained as tinnitus or low-frequency noise sensitivity, but there is more to it than that: this curious noise has been heard by non-sufferers of these condi-

tions like myself, and Gilbert White of Selbourne was familiar with it in the 18th century. The name "hummadruz" was given to this environmental sound during the 19th century. It was primarily associated with outdoor locations on still, hot summer days.

In August 1978, I was working with a council conservation team on restoring the footpaths that were to make up the Calderdale Way, near Halifax, West Yorkshire. One hot and sunny afternoon, after a bit of rain in the previous days, we had to clear a mass of holly trees from a trackway, and some of us also set about clearing wood, leaves and silt from a well-trough situated at a bend on the track on the wooded hillside.

While this was going on, I became aware of a buzzing sound, which I first thought to be the hum of woodland flies. Steadily, however, the noise became more intense; I looked round to try and locate the swarm of bees that I had assumed it to be, but could find no centre or direction to the sound. The other two people working on the well were also aware of the sound, but did not find it as loud or bothersome as I did; for me, the sound at its most intense seemed to be all around and inside my head, too. In the end, I went off outside the woodland to trim some holly instead. The sound was still there when we clocked off, but not on subsequent days. The location of this phenomenon was north of Halifax, near Catharine Slack – quite near a road, although not a very busy one. It was not a place where one would expect silence or any quietness beyond our contemporary normal background noise.

John Billingsley, Hebden Bridge, West Yorkshire, 1997

HUMDINGER

During the summer of 1994 while I was living in Oxfordshire, I was taken by a friend to an old forest known as The Wychwood (parts of which are alleged to have never been seen or touched by modern man) to search for burial mounds and other sites of interest. In one particularly old and untrodden patch of forest my friend told me to stop and asked me what I could hear. Much to my amazement, I heard a sound something between the buzzing of bees, the chattering of birds or possibly the sound of lots of children playing just beyond earshot, which if you're in the middle of The Wychwood is just not possible. The sound was accompanied by a bit of a floaty feeling. When I tried to hear the sound more clearly it faded and I found it was best heard when I just relaxed and let the sound float over me.

HEARING THINGS IT HAPPENED TO ME!

> " *The sound at its most intense seemed to be all around and inside my head* "

By and by we carried on our walk and eventually returned home. While I relaxed, the most curious sensation came over me: once again the same strange floaty feeling, but this time accompanied by an hallucination which looked like cine film coming off the end of its spool and flapping loose in the projector. My friend insisted that this was a normal side-effect of having visited such a place and that there are other such places the world over that would give rise to similar effects.
Matt Hatton, by email, 1998

HAUNTED WOODS
In May 1997, I was on a walking holiday along the South Downs Way (SDW) long distance path. One afternoon on a bright and windy day, I left the SDW and walked along a path that meandered downhill through a fairly open beechwood, towards the village of Cocking. Sitting on a fallen tree trunk to consult the map, I became aware of what seemed to be the sound of children laughing and shouting, coming from the direction I had just come from, although some distance away. The best description of the sound would be the noise from a school playground when heard from a distance. Expecting a bunch of rowdy youngsters to come tearing down the path at any moment, I continued to pour over the map. After about three or four minutes, I realised that the sound had not moved; it was still just out of earshot. Also, my head was spinning slightly, as if I had just stood up too fast, although I was still sitting on the trunk. Intrigued, I retraced my steps to the top of the hill. The higher I went, the less obvious the sound became, ceasing altogether when I reached the top. I had seen no one on the path, and the

IT HAPPENED TO ME! HEARING THINGS

SDW was deserted as far as I could see in both directions.

I would have put this experience down to an over-active imagination, but for my experience the next day. Walking in the Charlton Forest, just south of the SDW, I was forced to take shelter from a downpour under some rhododendron bushes. As the shower passed, I emerged to be confronted by the same sound as I had heard the previous day, only this time it seemed to be coming from all directions, and appeared to be louder than before. I scanned the surrounding woodland, and it was obvious that there were no children or anyone else in the area. After about five minutes or so, the sound gradually started to fade, to be replaced by the normal woodland noises of birdsong, etc. Again I felt light-headed.

Since then, whenever I have passed through any wooded areas, I have kept an ear open for these sounds, but without success, and I must admit to having no idea of their source. Dryads, maybe?
Kevin Groves, Brighton, Sussex, 1999

LOW FIDELITY

I have experienced the hummadruz in several sites in Derbyshire. The most striking occasion that I remember was sometime in the late 1960s near Robin Hood's Stride, near Winster, in the area the guidebooks refer to as The Dark Peak – although this name has only been coined fairly recently, presumably to differentiate between the grit stone area and the limestone area (The White Peak) where the rock is much paler. The ground was covered with short, fine twitch-like grass and bilberries, and the soil was thin. The noise worked up slowly until it became very loud indeed, and seemed to be all around rather than emanating from any specific direction. It almost felt as if the hillside itself were vibrating, yet it was not an unpleasant sensation. Slightly eerie, yes, and faintly disturbing, but actually quite a pleasant humming sound, like an orchestra tuning up, but on one note. In fact there did seem to be several notes, but blended together so that the overall effect was a single hum.

I am wondering now if the sound might be caused by the crystalline structure of the rocks resonating. It seems to be most prevalent in limestone, gritstone and granite areas. I would be interested to know if anyone has heard it in Charnwood Forest, for example, where there are very ancient rocks, including a crystalline form of granite; and also slates, which are highly resonant. As with other reports, I have only heard the sound in hot summer weather, but naturally I'm less likely to be hanging about in the Peak District in the dead of winter. Also close to

Robin Hood's Stride are several ancient sites, including standing stones, stone circles and a carved-out hermit's cave, all again seemingly connected with hummadruz (and popularly made from gritstone or granite).
Brenda Ray, Mickleover, Derby, 1998

BEEHIVE LANE
In the late Eighties I was working as a telephone engineer and had a call to a terraced house in Ilford, Essex, to check a noisy line. The man who answered the door appeared a bit stressed, so when I went in I immediately picked up the phone to listen for the noise. "No, no!" he said, "it's not on the line, just listen!" I could hear a low humming sound. The man explained that the noise was driving him and his family round the bend and he was trying to eliminate all possible causes. He said it seemed to permeate the whole house at night when it was quiet and they were trying to sleep. I disconnected the telephone line while he turned off the electricity mains, gas and water supply, but the noise remained. I then suggested it could be coming from next door. Luckily, he was on good terms with his neighbour and took me with him into her house which was only the thickness of a brick wall away. There was no noise at all. She obligingly turned off her services and we went back and checked in his house. The hum was still there. I suggested that he contact the local council, but he had already done so and the council experts were baffled. I never did find out what happened regarding this.

The oddest thing, I now realise, was the house's location. It was the first house in a turning off of Beehive Lane! This lane's title is very ancient. Perhaps the hummadruz was the original reason it was named so.
Ken Doughty, by email, 1999

MYSTERIOUS MUSIC AND VOICES

SIRENS
One mild evening in late November, I went for a walk and stopped by the old entrance of Cardiff's Roath dock, now disused. I smoked a cigarette and watched the full moon climbing the sky when I distinctly heard a baby's cry, piercing the regular noise of wind and water and flotsam. I tried to pinpoint it, but the sky had become cloudy, and artificial light didn't reach the water. It appeared to be

IT HAPPENED TO ME! HEARING THINGS

coming from the water, beyond the safety fence. For a moment, I felt like jumping the fence to investigate, but something made me turn away. After a few steps, the crying stopped, leaving only the sounds of tide and wind.

Suddenly I remembered that, as a child, an old sailor had told me that the seas hold many creatures, some of whom will save your life when the ship sinks, while others will lure you to destruction with love songs, enchantments, and calls of distress from dark places; so when the kind man goes over into the darkness to give help, he is taken away by these creatures – and bodies are never found.
Mario Dias, Cardiff, 2000

In the summer of 1998, when I was 15, I lived about two miles from Beulah, a small town in rural northern Michigan. I often used to bike down to a grimy old pond down the road and fish for a few hours in the evening, then head back when it got dark. One day as I was casting out, probably a good half hour before nightfall, there came a great gust of wind that sent a ripple right across the pond. The sky was a strange orange colour. I took a few steps back, but reeled in my line and cast as normal. Then I heard singing. It was a girl's voice, quite loud, which seemed to be coming from everywhere at once. There were no cars anywhere nearby so it wasn't coming from a radio. It was too loud and much too clear to be coming from a house. There were two houses fronting the pond, but no one was home at either that night. I was entirely alone.

It was a beautiful song, very comforting somehow. I couldn't understand the words, but they were definitely not English. It reminded me a bit of Amerindian music. This went on for 20 seconds or so and I remember putting my fishing rod down and having a sudden urge to jump into the water and swim out to the middle, feeling as if this would take me to another place. Instantly another feeling came over me, as if I were snapping back into my senses. I snatched my rod, picked up my bike, and peddled up the road faster than I ever had before. It was only a couple minutes back to my house, but in that time it began to rain quite hard. I burst into the kitchen and told my mother about the creepy music. She tried to calm me, even flipping on the radio and going through all the stations, but we couldn't find any type of music similar to what I had heard. I never returned to the pond; in fact I stopped fishing altogether that day.
Travis Wolfe, Grand Rapids, Michigan, 2005

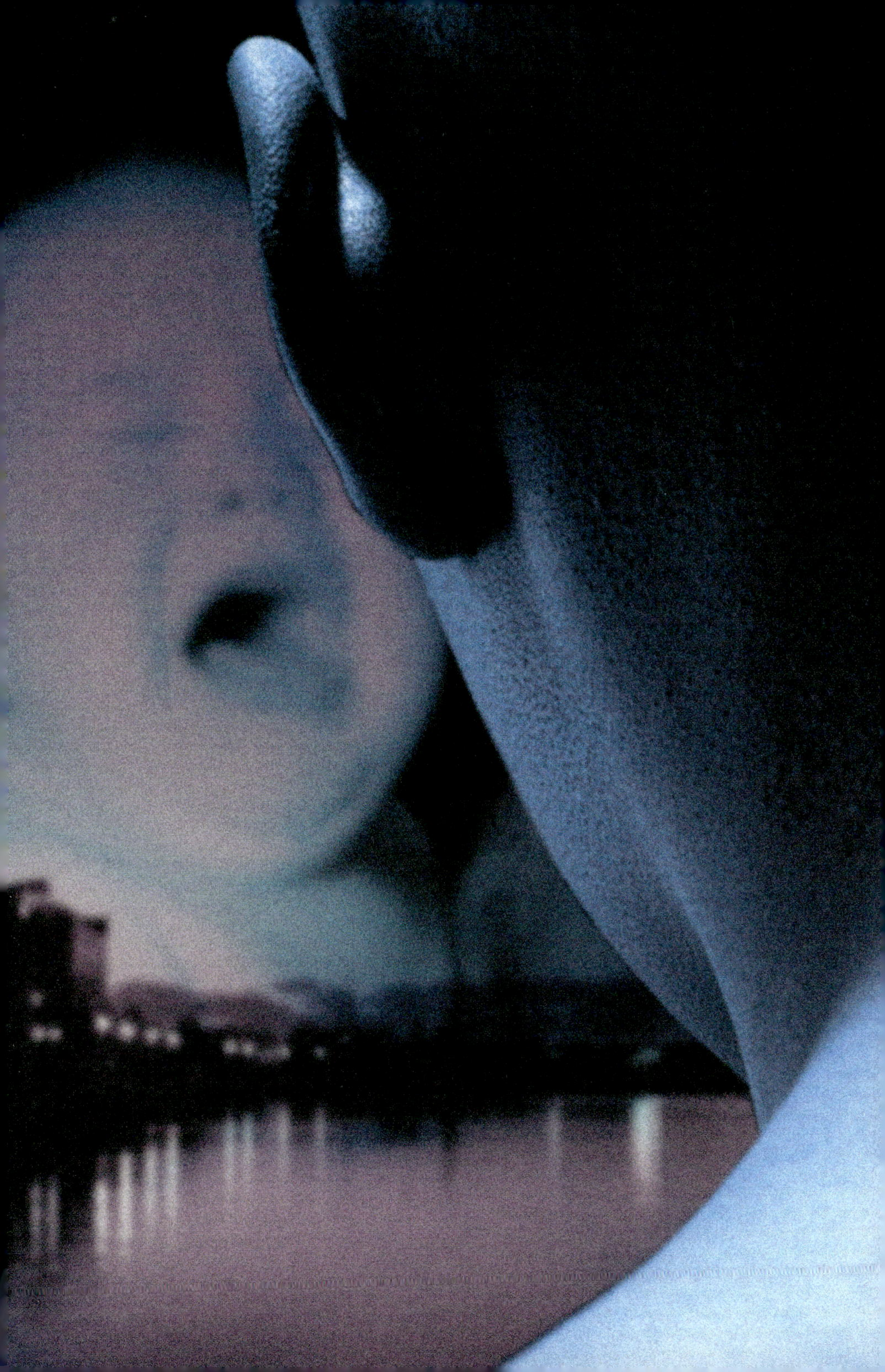

IT HAPPENED TO ME! HEARING THINGS

COUNTRY MUSIC

As a child of about seven, I was playing alone in the snow when I heard the most beautiful singing, first a solo voice, then joined by another in harmony. It grew louder and then faded away. Many years later I read a book by Elizabeth Goodge called *The Joy of the Snow*, where she writes about an identical experience. It had a profound effect on me, particularly as I have a gift for music, earning my living as a director of music in a school.

Three weeks after my husband died in May 1999, I was picking raspberries in the garden one evening when I heard the most glorious singing I have ever heard in my life, like a million people blending in the most exquisite harmonies. It lasted about a minute, faded, and then repeated about three hours later as I went upstairs to bed. I like to think that my beloved was allowed to send me just a little sample of what he was hearing to let me know that all was well with him.
Jacqueline L Spriggs, Mountfield, East Sussex, 2001

One late summer in the early 1990s, I visited Maiden Castle in Dorset with some friends. I went on ahead with my son and another child and stood on the entrance bank waiting for the rest of our party to come over from the car park. For the three or four minutes I was waiting I could hear the music of a pipe or flute, no particular tune, coming distantly from somewhere amongst the embankments. It was pleasing, but didn't have any particular effect. Alas, the children were too young to confirm this musical apparition.
Ed Griffiths, Prestwood, Buckinghamshire, 2001

JUNGLE CHEERING

In July 1994, my wife and I took a holiday in Cancun, Mexico. We decided to take a tour to the Mayan ruins at Chichén Itzá in northern Yucatan. Our bus journey took a good two hours through the jungle until we reached the large expanse of excavated ruins. Our guide told us to spend about half an hour looking through the orientation pavilion and then to congregate under the trees at the base of the large pyramid known locally as the Castillo. It was very hot and humid, so we were quite happy to gather under the shade of the trees in the large square.

As we stood there, I suddenly heard the sound of cheering from what sounded very much like a large arena. I was unable to discern the source of these thousands (?) of voices. The sound reminded me very much of being inside the confines of a football stadium. I tried to see if there were any loudspeakers

HEARING THINGS IT HAPPENED TO ME!

> " *I suddenly heard the sound of cheering from what sounded like a large arena...* "

responsible, but I knew that the sound was not coming from any one particular spot. It appeared that neither my wife nor anyone else was aware of what I could so clearly hear. The cheering lasted a good two minutes before stopping as abruptly as it had started.

Shortly afterwards, I discovered that close by was a ruin called The Temple of Warriors or The Temple of a Thousand Columns. Could this have been the source of the cheering (from the distant past)?
Graham Conway, Delta, British Columbia, 2003

ECHOES OF BATTLE

A NORMANDY TALE
A few miles west of Dieppe, in the woods above a cove, stands a small chateau, reputed to have been many things in its time, including the Wehrmacht headquarters in World War II. It is certainly an intriguing building, impressive without being imposing. If you make your way out of the back of the building and into the woods, you soon find a little stream that emerges after a few hundred metres onto a small beach. Like so many Normandy beaches, this one has a little sand and a lot of pebbles, and it is most likely to be empty, with just the sound of the waves breaking and perhaps the wind stirring the trees above. The once-busy port lies a few kilometres to the east, and to the west there is the lighthouse on

IT HAPPENED TO ME! HEARING THINGS

the headland.

I have twice visited the chateau during its spell as a residential centre for British schoolchildren, a role it has now ceased to fulfil. On my first stay, in the summer of 1981, I ended up sharing a room with a male teacher called Richard from a school in London. The pair of us, though strangers, were content with the arrangement, and as we were both fully occupied during the day, were keen on a good night's sleep whenever we could get it.

The second night was warm and the casement was open, a little breeze stirring the curtains as we dropped off to sleep around 11 o'clock. I was woken by a noise about an hour later. I thought at first that the window had banged in the breeze, but the breeze had dropped, and the partly drawn curtains were still. Then I heard the noise again, not close at all, but seeming to come from the woods beyond the chateau, or maybe even further away. It was a single loud bang, like a gunshot, and then, half a minute later, another. Poachers! I thought. I slipped back towards sleep, maybe for less than a minute, then I was wide awake again.

The single shots, for shots they surely were, were now coming more often, and in between there were bursts of machine-gun fire. It seemed no nearer, but it was louder, and appeared to come from several different places at once. Surely this could not be poachers, but in that case what was it? Now I could tell that Richard was awake too.

"What's all that?" he murmured.

"I don't know. Listen, do you think those are guns?"

"Sounds like it, doesn't it? But who's doing the shooting?"

"I've no idea."

We lay and listened. The sound grew but came no nearer, then it seemed to grow distant. Perhaps a wind was rising and blowing the sounds away? No, the curtains didn't stir, there was no noise of vehicles, no police sirens, no sound of commotion in the rooms around us.

At breakfast, there was no talk of war, battles in the night, or of any disturbance at all. According to the teachers, even the children had had a quiet night, something they found remarkable in itself. I had expected anxious talk of evacuation and concerns for our safety, but it started to dawn on me that nobody else had heard a thing. I caught Richard in the lobby before his party left for the day.

"So, have you spoken to anybody yet?" I asked.

"Yes, and I got a very strange reaction from the housekeeper, as though she had seen a ghost. Nobody else heard anything. So far it's just you and me that seem to know anything about all this at all."

When I told the organiser of the school trip on my return to England, she said that the stretch of coast nearby had had a turbulent history, and was the scene of a fierce battle during World War II. I looked this up in a history book and discovered that on 19 August 1942, a force of 5,000 Canadians, 1,000 British and 50 American Rangers attempted to take and hold the port of Dieppe. The raid was a high-risk operation and turned out to be a disaster. Of the 5,000 troops who got ashore, more than half were killed or captured, and the beach below our wood was a scene of very heavy fighting.

David Doughty, Loughborough, Leicestershire, 1997

SOUNDS OF BATTLE

My wife and I had a holiday in Dorset in 1977, during which we found an ideal picnic site just outside Cerne Abbas. It was a lovely sunny day, the entrance to a fallow field was ungated (it was posted as a bridle path) and nearby was a copse of trees perhaps some 10 to 15 metres (33-49ft) deep. Perfect. We spread our blanket and settled down to a read before our meal, when I became aware of a noise which at first I could not identify. It gradually increased in volume until I was quite certain what it was: a large number of horses and riders jostling together, the stamp of hooves, the snorting, creak of saddles, the chink of bridles.

The only place it could come from was the copse and, a bit nervously, I went to have a look. There was nothing and the sounds stopped. Nothing in the lane, and on the far side was a deserted garden. In the meantime, my wife went into the copse to answer a call of nature and came out as I returned to the car. She insisted that we move on, and all she could say was: "I don't know, but there's someone in there, someone was watching me." As we packed up our belongings, the odd sounds started again and we couldn't get away quickly enough. I mentioned this some years later to a friend whose family originated in Dorset, and he said that particular area was known to have been a battlefield in the Civil War.

Peter Brown, Slough, Berkshire, 2001

ROLE-GAME

12 The Twilight Zone

Some experiences are just so mind-bogglingly extraordinary that they are impossible to categorise. From a mysterious and menacing Mickey Mouse to a phantasmagorical pram with skittle-shaped passengers, from bouncing spook lights to a giant penguin that climbs out of a frame in the wall, we round off this collection with some truly out-of-this-world stories that defy understanding.

NOT QUITE HUMAN

THE CARPET SALESMAN
In 1965, I had just bought my first car, and took my wife and two daughters out into the country for a ride and picnic. Not far from here is a ruined castle and church, and in part of the church lies a crusader. My daughters wanted to see his tomb, and I lifted them up so that they could look inside through a grille in the door. Suddenly my wife screamed out in fright. A man had touched her on the shoulder. None of us had noticed his approach, even though the path and area we were standing on was covered in deep gravel.

The man was deeply upset and crying and I asked what was the matter. He asked us to follow him through the churchyard, which we did, then he asked us to go and read the inscription on a tombstone and return and tell him what the inscription said. The inscription read: "Here lies the body of Harold James Bell of Silloth, Cumberland. Born 21 June 1815. Died 21 June 1865, Aged 50 years."

On repeating this to the stranger, he broke down completely and after a while told us of this coincidence: he was Harold James Bell of Silloth, Cumberland. Born 21 June 1915; that day, 21 June 1965, was his 50th birthday. He was a sales rep for a Cumberland company, and had been asked on that day to travel east into this area where he had never been before. Five miles from here some unknown force took over control of the car and brought him off the main roads through a narrow country lane to this place. He had been pushed and shoved by something invisible until confronted by the tombstone.

He was convinced that the event was a way of showing him that he had come to the end of his natural life, and we could not convince him otherwise. My wife was really upset over the affair, and I decided we would leave. I escorted Mr Bell back to his car, noticed various credentials, carpet samples etc, and left.

Next Monday, I told the story to my manager at work. A week later he came to me with a laugh and complimented me on telling such a good story. He and his wife, walking in the area, decided to go and see the tombstone, and couldn't find it. I was amazed at this, as it really couldn't be missed. That evening after work I returned to the graveyard, and sure enough there was no gravestone, nor sign that it ever existed. My wife and I have revisited the site many times out of curiosity. I always wonder what became of the unhappy Mr Bell. Did he and his car really exist that day? Our conversation, the atmosphere and the unreality of it all made this the strangest happening in all my life.

Ron Parker, Middlesborough, Cleveland, 1980

SHE'S BEEN SLIMED!

One night in August 1994, a fellow police officer and I were patrolling the Queens Park area of Brighton in Sussex. Around 2am, we were asked to attend an incident outside the park gates. We found paramedics attempting to resuscitate an elderly woman who was lying by the roadside.

We were told that when found, the woman was covered in green slime, which appeared to have drowned her. There was plenty of this viscous ooze in evidence, both all over the woman and the attending medics. There was also a large amount in the gutter running some 20ft (6m) down the road. The old lady was taken to the nearby A&E where further attempts were made to revive her, which sadly were unsuccessful. When the lab examined the substance it was found to be "algæ-like" and apparently had been ingested in sufficient quantities to cause the woman's stomach to explode.

One theory bandied about was that the victim was a "hydromaniac" who had been drinking from the pond in the park and had staggered away only for the algæ to "ferment" inside her, expand, and cause the injury. However, her family denied any history of this type of activity, and were obviously distressed at this suggestion. We noticed the water level in the lake was low, and she would have

> **_The woman was covered in green slime, which seemed to have drowned her..._**

been obliged to climb into the muddy shallows and drink the stagnant water from the edge. There was no mud on her feet or hands, and no muddy footprints; and the slime didn't smell stagnant, but had a soapy smell not unlike detergent.
Mark Novell, by email, 2003

OUTLANDISH APPARITIONS

DISNEYFICATION OF TERROR
When the papers carry reports about people who claim to have seen creatures from space, I can accept the sincerity of those claims because of an experience I had when I was about five or six, almost 60 years ago. My grandparents lived in an old house with a very dark basement reached by a steep flight of steps behind a door. That was probably why my twin brother and I were forbidden even to open that door in their absence.

This was just what I did one day. Facing me was a very real, very solid figure filling the entire doorway. It gave me the fright of my life. I was looking at Mickey Mouse! When I was not much older and wiser, I knew that I couldn't possibly have seen a *fictional* character, but at that time – and to this day – the figure was very real.
Stanley Shoop, FRSC Elstree, Herts, 1992

RAPTURE OF THE DEEP

As well as being my birthday, 23 August had a special significance for me in 1971. I was serving with the Royal Air Force in Malta and most of my spare time was devoted to the excellent diving club, run strictly to British subaqua rules.

I was one of four instructors in the club of about 140 members and my immediate boss was an experienced diving officer called John, known affectionately as 'the old man of the sea'. An expedition was planned for a six-week period to explore the coast around Gozo, a small island off the coast. One of the sites chosen was a small inlet in Xlendi Bay, searching for Punic and Roman wrecks.

The initial dive on the site by myself and another instructor called Bob revealed that we would be diving at depths often in excess of 130ft (40m). As there was no decompression chamber on Gozo, strict diving procedures would have to be followed. We were testing out an Italian decompression meter which John thought was unreliable.

The descent to 130ft was uneventful and all was going to plan when Bob's demand valve started acting up, restricting his intake of air. Against all the rules, he indicated to me to stay down while he surfaced and sent down the standby diver to keep me company. I swam around for a while looking for anything of interest on the rocky ocean floor. I saw a light ahead of me and was drawn to it both by curiosity and by what seemed to be an unknown force.

Over the next ridge and much further down, I saw a very beautiful young woman, tall and slim, with a lovely figure, standing at the entrance to a large cave. She was dressed in what looked like a white Indian sari; she wore sandals, her hair was plaited, and her wrists were adorned with various bracelets. The incandescence of the surrounding area added to the serenity and calm of the sight before me.

I thought that I must be suffering from 'the narcs', nitrogen narcosis, described in the early days of diving as 'the rapture of the deep', a feeling of euphoria, closely resembling drunkenness. As a very experienced instructor with more than 200 deep dives under my belt I realised that I was in deep trouble, deep being the operative word.

A look at my depth gauge revealed that I was 230ft (70m) down. The Italian decompression meter strapped to my wrist had long since given up as it was full of water. Fascination at what I saw overruled my training and my immediate need for an ascent and decompression procedures.

Then she spoke. "Hello, I have been waiting for you. o not be afraid, I mean you no harm, with me you are safe". I backed away, but she smiled, walked towards me and held out her hand. It felt warm, sensual and safe, and my fear disappeared.

"When you return to me I will be waiting for you, then you will stay with me forever. I have a gift for you". She handed me a small jar about 5in (13cm) tall, shaped like an amphora, which I took from her with my other hand. "Now you must go. You will always be safe for your return to me," she said. As I ascended, I saw her waving as she slowly faded from view into the azure depth. After a very long decompression stop aided by a spare set of air cylinders it was explanation time: the needle on the depth gauge registered 235ft (72m).

"Faulty gauge," said John, "because if it isn't you are in a lot of trouble; with that sort of depth on the clock you had better stay within camp area and keep someone with you in case of any bends problem."

About one week later I was summoned by John, who told me that the depth gauge had been tested and was completely accurate and serviceable, making my dive the longest and deepest in club history. Why I did not get the bends was a mystery to him. He also told me that Mr Mallia, the curator of the archaeological section of the Malta national museum, had identified the jar I had retrieved as a Phoenician scent jar of about 2000BC, used by the royal ladies of that time. The mystery was that its contents still smelled fresh, the potter's stamp on the side of the handle was crystal clear and the jar was described in the report as being in mint condition. John was curious where I had got it. "You wouldn't believe me if I told you," I said.

In September 1995, I revisited Xlendi Bay and swam out to the entrance of the bay for old time's sake. The next day, on my return to England, I suffered a severe heart attack. I was very fortunate to survive.

Ian Skinner, Hull, Humberside, 1996

FENCE FIEND

Five years ago two friends told me about a ghost they had seen on a suburban road in Bradwell (near Great Yarmouth, Norfolk). Interested but sceptical, I went with them the following night to a passage that bisects a block of houses about two minutes from where I live. They described a "tall man" who would appear at the end of this passage. It was dark, but visibility was good thanks to ample street lighting.

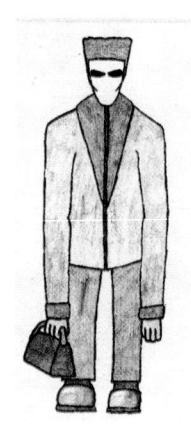

I was told to stare hard at a fence 20ft (6m) away, where I could instantly see movement. After a few minutes an apparition came plainly into view. It was humanoid, at least 7ft (2m) tall and wearing dark, heavy clothing (see drawing). It had a white, pear-shaped head with two dark eye sockets as its only features. The head was topped by tight orange hair, flat on top, which gave the face the appearance of being an upside-down triangle. Its arms were very long, almost touching the ground, and it carried a black doctor's bag in one of its gloved hands.

Despite its malignant appearance, I didn't feel afraid and watched as it repeatedly took one step forward and then return to its previous position, like a projection. It faded after about 10 minutes and my friends commented on how much clearer it was than when they had seen it the night before. One of them was terrified and suffered nightmares for weeks afterwards.

I returned several times, but despite feeling uneasy, I never saw it again.
Karl Thornley, Corleston, Norfolk, 1998

GRAVEYARD VISION

In the summer of 1998, I think it was Saturday 27 June, I was out driving around with two friends, and we decided to take some back roads to see where they went. We were in Ohio, driving down State Route 141 from Gallipolis to Oak Hill. We turned off 141 onto 233, and after a couple of miles we saw a country road leading off to the right. None of us knew where it went, so we took it. It was just before sunset. After about a mile, the road became much darker because of a wall of tall pine trees that lined both sides. Half a mile further on, we came to a clearing in the woods to the right.

The road came to a dead-end just past the clearing, so we decided to get out and look around. An old church stood at the base of a slight incline, looking as if

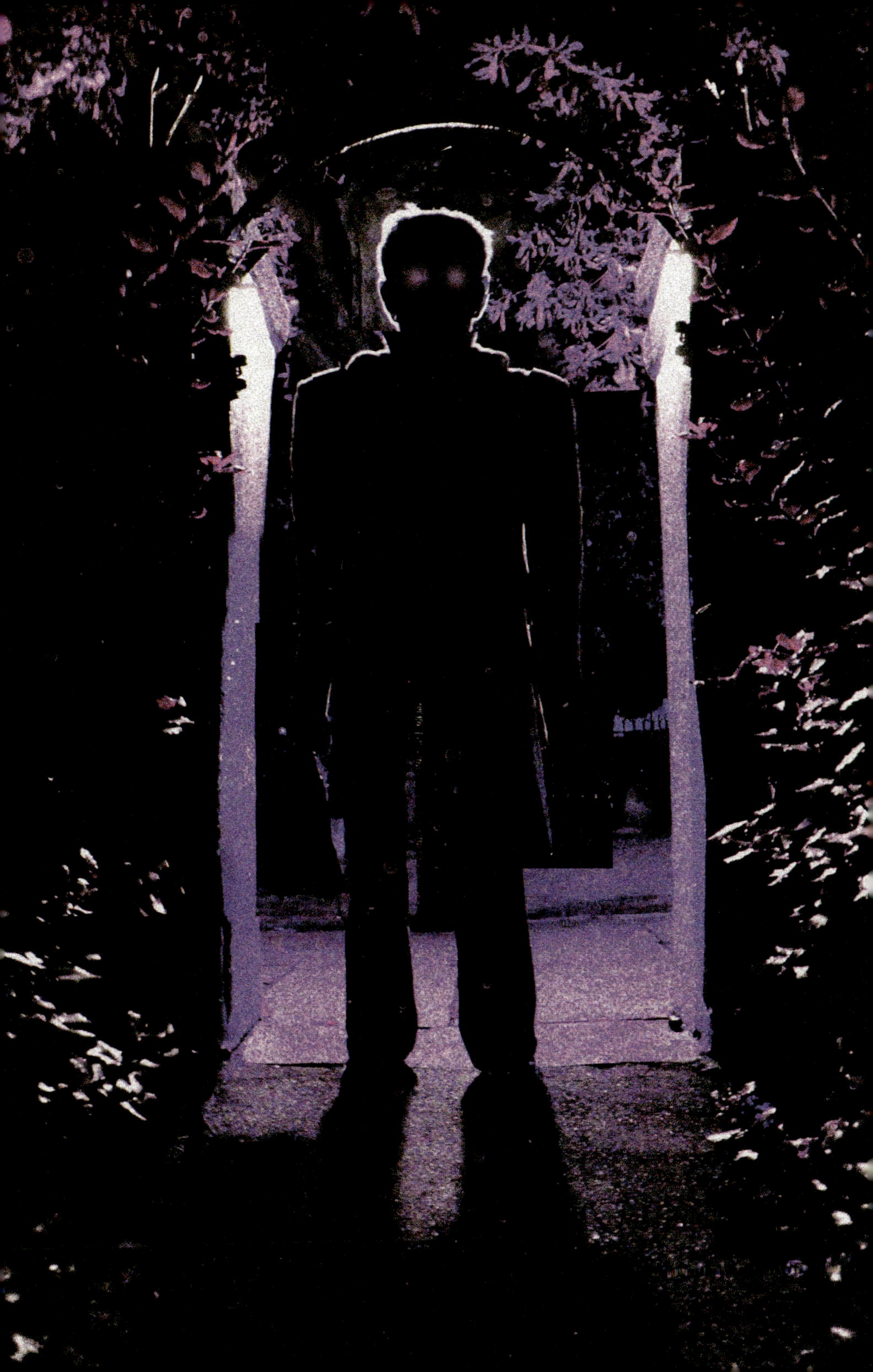

it hadn't been used in decades, but not in bad condition. A cemetery stretched out up the hill behind the church. At the top of the hill, there were two tombs with large, concrete slabs. My friends and I looked around the church, and then walked up the hill. By this time the cemetery was starting to get pretty dark, so we sat down by the tombs and looked around at the surrounding area. After about a half an hour, we decided to walk back to the car.

As we walked down the hill, my friend Brad was commenting on how large the tombstones were when all three of us noticed a black, man-sized shape rise up from behind the tombstone that we were looking at, less than 10ft (3m) away. Brad stopped dead in his tracks and started to freak out, because this thing was standing right in front of him, with its 'hands' on the top of the tombstone, just staring at us. It was like looking at a void. You could almost see through the shape, but it still appeared to be almost solid. I grabbed Brad's arm and pulled him towards the car.

My friend Matt, on my left, saw the figure as well, and started walking, almost running, towards the car. The shape ran up the hill towards the area where we had been sitting, but when it reached a tombstone before those at the top, it disappeared behind it, as if it had dropped down into a grave. Needless to say, we left in a hurry. Brad, who is a devout Christian and doesn't believe in ghosts, was on the verge of a breakdown, saying, "Oh my God! Oh my God! What was that? Oh my God!" The three of us were all genuinely scared.

We decided to go back to the area the next day to get a clearer look and to search for footprints (thinking that someone might have played a really clever trick on us). When we passed the rows of pines and made it to the clearing, we couldn't believe our eyes. The abandoned church was now in ashes on the ground, smoke still rising from its foundation. Most of the tombstones had been turned over and were lying on the ground. Some of these were too large for one person, or even four or five people to budge, and would've taken a machine of some sort to actually push them over.

Andrew Beattie, by email, 2006

BEDSIDE VISITOR

Around 2:30 or so one morning 11 years ago, when I was around 15 years old, I put down the book I was reading, got under the covers, and switched off my reading light. As I was setting down my glasses on the bedside table, I noticed that my room had become very warm, almost oppressively so. I felt very uncomfortable

THE TWILIGHT ZONE IT HAPPENED TO ME!

" When I awoke, my pillow and bedclothes were soaked with blood... "

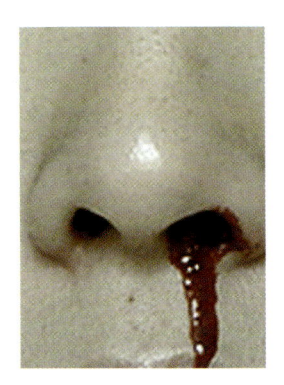

and vulnerable – so I reached for my glasses again. The lenses were fogged and I used my pillowcase to wipe off the condensation. I looked around but saw nothing unusual, so I kicked off the covers and began to relax.

After about maybe 30 seconds, I heard a vibration, fast and buzzing like a muted cell phone. The volume increased at least tenfold and was joined by an almost metallic-sounding whine. The vibration was so loud the glass in my bedroom window was shaking violently, almost to the point where I felt it would shatter. An enormous pressure began to build around me, as if I were on a rollercoaster, and the fillings in my two back teeth started to get very hot.

Then, to my horror, the air to the right of my bed expanded like a soap bubble being blown and revealed a tall, completely white figure that was very thin, almost two-dimensional, and featureless. The figure pushed violently against the air around the 'soap bubble' as if it were pushing through a balloon, and distorted the air like a funhouse mirror. At this point I tried to scream, but the vibration completely drowned out any noise I tried to make. The figure then started whipping and thrashing harder than ever, and the pressure around me increased so much that I started to get blurred vision. After a short time – I don't know how long for sure as there wasn't a clock in my line of sight – I lost consciousness.

When I awoke at around 3:30am, my pillow and bedclothes were soaked with blood from my nose, and I had a horrible headache from the back of my eyes to the top of my head. I went into my mother's room to tell her that I didn't feel good. My mother, who was awake, took one look at all the blood on me and immediately made my stepfather drive me to the hospital.

On the way, I asked her why she was awake. She wouldn't give me a straight

153

answer but mentioned something about a loud noise. She was recovering from a stroke at the time, so it was hard for her to describe things. My stepfather was visibly shaken and wouldn't look me in the eyes when I described what happened.

We arrived at the hospital and they gave me a CAT scan (I think they did anyway) and other tests. The doctor kept asking me if we had flown on a plane, or been anywhere with high elevation within the last day or so – which of course we hadn't. I was sent home with some mild pain relievers and a clean bill of health.
Dustin Hiles, Indianapolis, Indiana, 2006

LISTEN TO THE PENGUIN

When I was about six, in 1958 or thereabouts, I had an experience which has stayed with me ever since. In those days I often shared my parents' bed, sleeping in the delicious safety and warmth between their bodies. One night I awoke and, looking down past the foot of the bed towards the built-in wardrobes, I saw a circle of light apparently projected on the doors. The circle grew until it was about three feet in diameter, at which point a face appeared in it and began to give a news summary or similar kind of account; I received the distinct impression that this, whatever it was the man was talking about, was merely the preamble to some unknown main business.

After a few moments the talking head announced that "the moment you've been waiting for" had arrived and proceeded to introduce "the penguin". This turned out to be nothing less than a giant (ie. adult-sized) bird which promptly climbed out of the frame on the wall and waddled around the end of the bed on my mother's side. Leaning over her sleeping body, of which I was perfectly aware and wondering why she didn't wake up with all the noise, it poked its beak in my face and told me that if I didn't start eating my crusts (something my mother had constantly nagged me to do) it would return and eat me!

The penguin then climbed back into the frame, there was a final burst of music and the light went out. Only then was I able to move to shake my mother awake and tell her the whole terrifying story. I remember she insisted it was all a dream – naturally. But I also recall that at the time there was absolutely no division between this event and waking events. I believed totally in the reality of that penguin and the seriousness of its message. In fact I accepted the incident as real for probably more than 20 years; had someone asked me if I had really been visited by a nocturnal flightless bird with an interest in my eating bread crusts, I would unhesitatingly have said yes.

I recall the event, whatever it was, often and always manage to summon up the feeling of apprehension and fear which went with it. Like most children, I accepted the world the way adults said it was, I accepted their authority. Perhaps the penguin was some subconscious manifestation stemming from guilt at not obeying Mum's constant reminders to eat my crusts. But why a penguin, of all things? Why the chat show format years before the invention of chat shows? The whole thing was in full colour, years before colour TV.

There is the possibility that the penguin was a waking dream. Reason demands the question: what else could it be? It's too trivial, too silly to be anything significant. Still, I always ate my crusts after that night.

Anthony Purcell, Chelmsford, Essex, 1997

MYSTERIOUS LIGHTS

THE FIREBALL

During World War II, I was staying with my grandparents here in Stokesley (near Middlesborough). They lived in a small cottage by the river, and one day we had a thunderstorm. My grandparents went to every room in the house opening every door and window, "so if the lightning comes in it can get out again." We were all sitting in the small back room when there came the biggest flash of lightning and peal of thunder that I have ever heard, and above the sound of pouring rain we heard a loud fizzing sound. I went to the back door and there on the step was this football-sized blue bubble which seemed to be spinning on its axis at a terrific rate of knots.

The draft caused the bubble to be drawn into the room, where it floated gently into all four corners, passing under the table twice. It did not seem to emit any heat, although it fizzed and crackled and was nearly of blinding intensity. At this time we were all standing on chairs. The cutlery in the table drawer was all magnetised together.

The bubble was then caught in the through draft and left via the sitting room and front door, and as it passed the electricity meter behind the front door exploded. The bubble then gained height and speed, sped away in a great curve and

smashed into the roof of a house 300 yards (275m) away. We were really alarmed at the explosion and amount of damage caused by our visitor, which seemed to us to have no more substance than a penny balloon.
Ron Parker, Middlesborough, Cleveland, 1980

OKLAHOMA SPOOK LIGHTS
I was born and bred in Miami, in the north-east corner of the state of Oklahoma, where the government herded all the Indians around 1905. Here are situated the 1930s boom towns of Cardin and Pitcher, known as the badlands, where Bonnie and Clyde holed out when they weren't killing people. After World War II the lead and zinc mines closed down and the towns declined. By 1970, the population of Cardin had dropped from 20,000 to under 100, and that of Pitcher from 30,000 to 200. The area is full of ruins and deserted roads, and is honeycombed with mines which tend to collapse, leaving large holes in the ground.

Near the small town of Quapaw is a large Indian reservation, which has its own spook light, reputedly known to the Indians before the white man arrived. It appears on a lonely country road with few houses. My father told me it was much more pronounced in the '40s and '50s before a highway was built close by. One time he and his brothers went to see it, and after waiting a while they saw it appear down the road. As they watched it, it seemed to get larger and rolled down the road towards them. Shaken, they jumped in the car and the light passed straight through the car. When they turned around to watch it, it was gone.

I saw the light many times when I was young. It was well known, and generally there was a crowd watching for it, but it was usually a long way away. There was a small, run-down museum with old clippings about scientific studies made on the light in the '30s and '40s. In 1973 I moved to Nashville, but returned to visit the following year. On Hallowe'en night I drove out with my cousins Ken, Roy and Sherry to check out the spook light. We parked and waited in the rain. At about 2am we saw it bouncing back and forth across the road, at a guess about half a mile away. As we watched, it split in two and started crossing itself as it bounced. My father told me he had seen it do this. Suddenly it disappeared, and after a few minutes it appeared in the woods right next to the car. Then something hit the roof of the car. This scared us, and we drove away fast. This is the first time I have written about this, and I still get cold chills thinking about it.
Paul Moss, Nashville, Tennessee, 1989

> **The sun was enlarged and spinning around really fast like a Catherine Wheel**

SPINNING SUN

In September 1983 or 1984, when I was 11 or 12, my mum and I went on an organised coach trip with loads of other people from our Catholic diocese to Hazelwood Castle, near York. The point of the excursion was to meet other religious folk there and pray for world peace.

In the early evening after we'd finished praying we went into the car park to board the coach. I looked up into the sky and saw the Sun, which was rather enlarged, spinning around really fast like a Catherine wheel. Sparks were flying off it and it changed to blue, green, red, purple, and all the colours of the rainbow. I couldn't take my eyes off it. It didn't hurt to look at it – in fact, it almost seemed to soothe my eyes in a kind of blissful way and I was hypnotised by its beauty. My mum kept telling me to stop looking at it but I couldn't. I kept saying "But it doesn't hurt your eyes! Look at it!" But she wouldn't stare at it, even though she knew it was happening.

Eventually she managed to drag me onto the coach and I ran to the back so I could keep on staring at it through the rear window. I must have looked at it for about half an hour, but I've no eye damage. When we'd travelled a fair bit, the Sun went out of view and when I saw it again it was back to its usual self and hurt when I looked at it.

Both my mum and I remember the event very clearly, although we can't remember the date. Everyone thinks we're bonkers.

Julia Burns, Keighley, West Yorkshire, 2002

CHASED BY BALL LIGHTNING

When I was about 12 years old, I lived with my family in a semi-detached house in Hampshire with no overhead power lines nearby. One beautiful clear summer afternoon, without a cloud in the sky and no hint of thunderstorms, I was in the living room doing a school assignment; my mother and great grandmother were in the kitchen cleaning. The only electrical appliance on in the house was a small battery-powered radio. The letterbox rattled and, thinking we had post, I put down my books and went to see. At that moment, a blinding ball of blue-white light floated lazily into the living room and hovered about a meter away from me at head height for several seconds. I made a break for the door and ran into the kitchen with my hair standing on end.

A few seconds later the ball of light (BOL) bobbed and danced its way into the kitchen and hovered over my head. It seemed to like me. "Bugger me!" exclaimed my mother and my great gran threw a tea towel over her head and shrieked, "Don't panic!" At this point the BOL wandered out of the back door into the garden and vanished. The whole incident took about a minute.

Ever since that day I seem to have had an inherent ability to trash electrical equipment just by touching it or even just looking at it. I can arc lightning across my cat's ears (he hates it, but I don't do it on purpose). My partner won't let me anywhere near his electronics equipment and I still suffer from really, really bad hair days.

Kirsten Cross, Bampton, Devon, 2003

EXTRAORDINARY OBJECTS

CUP-CAKE PRAM?

I must tell you of a mysterious object which I encountered in June 1975.

I recall sitting on the grass of our local park, in Grimsby, one night with a schoolfriend. From where we were sitting, at the very edge of a large expanse of lawn used for bowling, we had a clear view of Park Drive to our right, its stretch broken here and there by clumps of trees.

It was definitely fully dark – though I forget what time – when an object came into view, travelling left to right along Park Drive and in full illumination of the street lights. I estimate our distance from the road to be no more than 30 yards

THE TWILIGHT ZONE IT HAPPENED TO ME!

(27m) – I frequently revisit this spot so I am pretty sure of the distance – yet for some strange reason, we could not make optical sense of the object we both turned to look at.

Firstly, it was luminous white and its edges were blurred, while it travelled about walking speed along the centre of the road. The main body of the object resembled a large pram without wheels. At each end of the 'pram' was seated a figure, featureless and white; in fact they were hardly figures at all, but more like skittles or milk bottles with rounded 'heads' [*see accompanying sketch*].

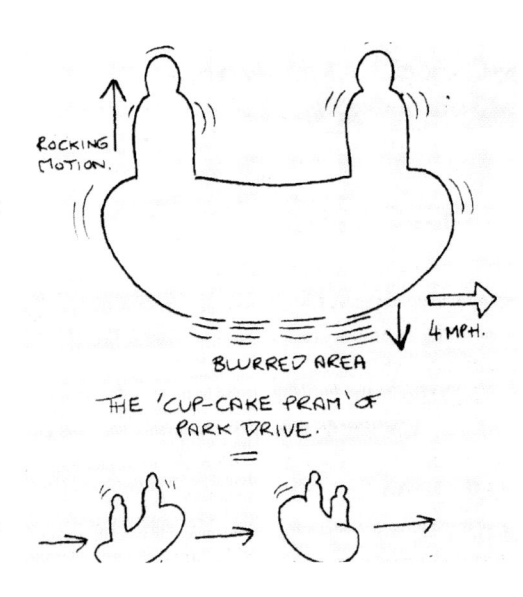

The most alarming aspect of the object and occupants was the way they rocked up and down in see-saw fashion, in unison with the carriage. There was no one pushing this object, and it was devoid of superstructure (handle, hood, wheels, etc). It did not hover above the ground, but seemed to blur into the ground where the wheels should be.

We watched it for around two minutes before it disappeared behind trees – it may have turned into a driveway at that point – and never reappeared.

Strangely, and I still can't understand why, we never gave chase for a closer look – we just gazed at the object in bemused acceptance.
Art Wetherell, Stallingborough, South Humerside, 1992

TAPPING THE HEAD FIELD
In the early 1960s, I was at a special boarding school for the deaf at Bolton near Manchester. Sometime between 1964 and 1966, on a summer evening around 4.30pm, I was standing alone in the school's washroom. Because I was small, I was standing on a wooden chair so that I could look in the mirror to brush my

hair. As I turned the cold water tap on to wet my hair, a horrible vibrating noise made me think there must be an airlock in the pipes. I ran the comb under the water and raised it towards my hair, but it hit something solid above my head. I looked up to see what it was and was frightened to find nothing there. The ceiling was about 15ft (4.6m) high, so I tried once more to comb my hair. Again it hit something a few inches above my head, and again when I looked there was nothing there. I raised my hand and pressed against what felt like glass or an invisible force field.

I ran into the corridor trying to find someone to witness this phenomenon – but there was no one around. I was excited as well as scared and so I returned to the chair, stood on it again and hit the barrier as hard as I could with the hope of smashing it, but all it did was make a dull thud that echoed around the washroom. I then became frightened that it would crush me to death, so I turned off the running tap and was about to leave when I realised that the barrier had vanished. I turned the tap on again but it did not come back. I tried numerous 'settings' on the tap for the rest of my time at the school, but the barrier never happened again.

Karl Liggett, Newton-le-Willows, Merseyside, 1997

AIDA AND THE ROLLING STONES

In 1970 I was an eight-year-old girl in a family of four, and together with my parents, an aunt, an uncle, and a servant girl called Aida, lived in a big wooden house in the Philippines with my maternal grandparents.

One evening around Easter, we were all invited over by my paternal grandparents who lived nearby. As grandpa was having bouts of sinusitis he stayed behind, along with his wife and Aida. After a while, grandpa came over, panting and visibly shaken. He told us to come home at once as something strange was happening to Aida.

We hurried back amid a slight shower. Aida and my grandmother were huddled in the middle of the house, hugging each other. Our 17-year-old servant girl was crying hysterically. She came from a poor family in a faraway village and had been with us for about three years. She was tough and very determined, not easily scared. All of us children adored her.

Grandpa pointed to the stones forming a circle around the two women. He said it all started half an hour earlier when, out of nowhere, stones came rolling towards Aida. Black and smooth, mostly about one inch (2.5cm) in diameter and with varying oval shapes, they stopped a few inches from her feet. Just then, Aida screamed as another stone came rolling across the shiny wooden floor. All of us children became equally frightened and some started crying. All the doors were closed and all the windows screened. Behind the house were tropical trees and acres of paddy fields. There was no possible entry.

The stones kept rolling, following Aida wherever she went. They came from different directions and at different time intervals, as if the thrower was playing with us. I will never forget the sound of them rolling on the wooden floor. Gradually overcoming our fright, we children started to collect the stones in a vase. There were none like them in our neighbourhood. They were warm to the touch, and dry. Had they been thrown from the street outside, they would have been wet from the rain. The adults checked the house meticulously, and a neighbour let one of his hired hands go up into the ceiling to investigate, but he came back empty-handed.

That night, Aida slept on the floor of my grandparents' room, too scared to stay on her own. All through the night, we could hear the stones rolling and Aida's occasional whimper. In the morning, the mosquito net under which she slept was surrounded by stones. Nothing happened during the day, but the stones resumed rolling at sunset, as they did for the next two weeks.

As Easter approached, only about 10 stones appeared nightly, compared to 20 or 30 previously. Many people came and asked for a stone or two, thinking they were from out of this world and would bring them luck. Being Catholic, my family held daily prayer meetings and the local parish priest blessed the house. He was convinced that evil spirits were at work.

Then my mother met an old wise man in the market place, and told him of the phenomenon. He said that Aida was being befriended by a playful gnome who wanted to attract her attention. Such creatures were invisible and usually harmless. To stop the stones, he advised that salt be spread outside around the house at sunset. Reasoning that she had nothing to lose, my mother followed his instructions. She and my aunt started at the bottom of the front stairs and spread salt in opposite directions until they met at the back of the house. Much to everyone's relief, the stones stopped appearing.

Aida stayed with us for another two years and then moved to the city, taking with her a few of the stones that for two weeks had made her life something to be remembered by all who knew her.

Darcy Frederiksen, Tripoli, Libya, 1999

Fortean Times would like to thank all those who have written to us to share their experiences over the past 35 years. A particular thank you goes to those writers whose letters appear in this volume:

Amos --, SJ Adams, Colin Ayling, Tony Baldwin, J Bardet, Joseph E Barnes, Andrew Beattie, Mary Behrens, John Billingsley, John Birch, Alex Brattell, Peter Brown, Julia Burns, Deborah Cameron, Emma Cannell, Mrs M Carroll, Simon Clabby, Sheila Clark, Amanda-Jayne Clayden, Darren E Companion, Graham Conway, Roy C Cotterill, Andrew Cray, Donald Crighton, Kes Cross, Kirsten Cross, Alun Cureton, AG Russell-Dallamore, Jamie Davis, Simon Day, Ian Deakin, Eileen Denham, Alison Derrick, Mario Dias, Rob Dickinson, Malcolm Dickson, David Doughty, Ken Doughty, Gunnar Th Eggertsson, Phillip A Ellis, Phillip Evans, Joy Ferguson, Christopher Fowler, Darcy Frederiksen, Rob Gandy, Cyrus Ganjavi, Martin Garcia, Judith Gee, Derek Gibson, Jerry Glover, Derek Gosling, Rose-Mary Gower, Darren Green, Mrs JM Green, Norman Green, Doreen Greenwood, Ed Griffiths, Kevin Groves, DA Haines, Mike Harding, Linda Hardy, Matt Hatton, Margaret Hickey, Dustin Hiles, Graham Hill, Philip Hoare, Viv Hobbs, Andy Hinkinson-Hodnett, Rebecca Hough, Nic Johnson, Alex Jones, Mr J Keen, Chris Kershaw, Ms KJ Kimberly, Rob Kirbyson, John Knifton, Mrs E Knight, Patricia Law, Karl Liggett, Peter Lloyd, Francis Lowe, Tracey Maclean, John MacLeod, Keith Manies, Sharon Mason, Lily Mayhew, Christopher McDermott, Michael Mcquate, Neil Fielder-Mennell, Alan Moore, Tania Morgan, Paul Moss, Robert Moyes, Mazda Munn, Elias Paul Mutwira, Martin Nield, Mervyn FW Nightingale, Mark Novell, Kayti Ooi, Mike Owens, Ron Parker, Brian Perryman, Colby Pope, Wayne Poulsen, Anthony Purcell, Brenda Ray, Valerie Redgrave, Valerie A Riddell, John D Ritchie, John Robinson, Jack Romano, Ron Rosenblatt, AT Ryland, Matthew Salt, CN Satterthwaite, Nicola Savage, Darren R Scothern, Chris Shilling, Stanley Shoop, Mrs DJ Singleton, Ian Skinner, SA Skinner, Anna Smith, Anthony Smith, Euan Smith, Jacqueline L Spriggs, Lee Stansfield, Peter Sutherland, Robin Swope, Josephine Taylor, Karl Thornley, Pam Thornton, Clive Thrower, Patricia Tyrrell, LU, Steve Uzzell, David Le Vay, SW, Art Wetherell, Russ Williams, Travis Wolfe, James XXX, Rod York, Dr P Young, David Zanotti, Peter Zolli

FOR MORE REAL-LIFE STORIES OF THE UNEXPLAINED, SIGN UP TO THE *FORTEAN TIMES* MESSAGE BOARD AT WWW.FORTEANTIMES.COM/FORUM AND VISIT THE 'IT HAPPENED TO ME!' FORUM.

IF YOU HAVE YOUR OWN BIZARRE STORIES TO TELL AND WOULD LIKE TO SHARE THEM WITH US, THEN SEND YOUR LETTERS TO P.O. BOX 2409 LONDON NW5 4NP OR EMAIL SIEVEKING@FORTEANTIMES.COM